D0915907

THE SEAMLESS SEAT

THE SEAMLESS SEAT

CREATING THE IDEAL CONNECTION WITH YOUR HORSE

Kathleen Schmitt

THE LYONS PRESS

Guilford, Connecticut

An imprint of The Globe Pequot Press

The Lyons Press is an imprint of The Globe Pequot Press

10 9 8 7 6 5 4 3 2 1

Printed in the United States of America

Designed by Sheryl P. Kober

ISBN-13: 978-1-59228-685-0
ISBN-10: 1-59228-685-2

Library of Congress Cataloging-in-Publication Data is available on file.

To all horses, each of whom teaches me something new,
but especially to Beau Regarde,
whose student I was fortunate enough to be
for twenty-seven years.

CONTENTS

INTRODUCTION

There was once a boy who banged a drum all day and loved every moment of it. He wouldn't be quiet no matter what anyone did. Wise men tried all sorts of things. One threatened to perforate the boy's eardrums. Another said drum-beating was sacred and only for special occasions. A third offered neighbors plugs for their ears. A fourth gave the boy a book. A fifth gave the neighbors books about controlling anger through biofeedback. A sixth gave the boy meditation exercises. Nothing worked for very long.

The seventh wise man gave the boy a hammer and chisel and said, "I wonder what is inside the drum?"

—SUFI STORY

WHAT IS IT LIKE TO BE A GOOD RIDER?

Our first thought in riding is not always about how our riding feels to our horse. More often, we are concerned with our security and getting the horse to do what we want it to do. But considering what the horse considers important, perhaps even of interest, in our dealings with them can result in a tremendous improvement in the horse's performance and our own comfort.

Riders, like leaders in any partnership, get better results when the job is rewarding for those carrying out the orders. The leading partner might be surprised to learn some of the reasons the performing partner enjoys a job (or not), but certainly the performing partner will prefer to understand the task and be physically fit enough for it. I find horses hold enjoying life in general as a very high goal, so I find it is worthwhile to arrange for horses to enjoy the jobs we give them to do, even when they sometimes call on the horse's utmost will and strength. There is certainly joy in achievement for both horse and human.

Sjem looking forward to the next jump, and Jerome Dubbledam looking at Olympic Gold.

Horses have much to learn about what we want them to do and how we communicate that, and they are generally excellent at learning what we teach them. Just like we take a keen interest in our leaders at our jobs or school, horses learn to understand their riders very well, often far better than we appreciate at the moment. But just as good leaders understand the job and see to it those getting the job done have the needed physical skills and knowledge, it is up to riders to understand how well each horse's current abilities and interests match the job at hand. Riders also need the physical and personal skills to convey our plans and understanding to the horse, so we can develop the horse's natural abilities in good health.

Then, each species' unique talents can blend to produce the best possible performance in any riding sport. Then, riders' and horses' goals can become remarkably compatible for species that are basically so very different from each other.

There is a lot for humans to learn in order to ride well, too. It can even be tough to figure out what good riding is like.

Two of the common instructions given in any riding sport are some version of "heels down, hands down, head up" and "keep your horse moving forward." Yet we see these basic instructions apparently violated even at the highest levels of riding in any sport.

There may be perfectly good reasons a rider might intentionally go against these generally accepted directives. Heels coming up or hands being raised on purpose is one thing; it is quite another matter when riders do not mean to do it, do not realize it is happening, or meant to do something different.

Horses feel exactly what we do, whether or not we mean to pull our heels up, lift our hands, look down, or allow the horse's forward drive to trickle into nothing. We would feel all these things just as accurately as horses do if we were in the horse's position: at the receiving end of everything riders do. What we don't know about our riding is just the sort of thing that can cause the horse to do things we don't expect or understand.

But getting an idea of how a horse experiences us as riders might be rather easy. It is probably a lot like when we carry someone piggyback.

When we carry a child piggyback, we know when he makes any movement at all. We can probably even tell when he swallows or takes a breath. The child is probably just enjoying the ride and not much considering how she feels to the person carrying her. And when we carry a child piggyback, we usually don't interpret movements as commands or signals . . . but what if we did?

I wonder how long it would take a child being carried piggyback to figure out what you were up to if you turned left when the kid shifted their weight to the left and turned right when the kid shifted to the right. That would be easier than keeping in a straight line when the child shifts its weight, anyway. How would a game like that change what you and the child pay attention to as you walk along? What would it take for you and the child to wordlessly work out an agreement about how you influence each other? When might you decide to "break the rules" you had worked out?

There's a good chance that the child will eventually shift left or right without meaning for you to turn. What's likely to happen then? What's likely to happen if the child is holding a string attached to a piece of metal in your mouth? What if they also have pieces of pointy metal attached to their heels?

To know what it takes to be a good rider yourself, all you have to do is imagine what you would want from a person you are carrying piggyback when she is in charge of things.

RIDERS HAVE THREE MAIN JOBS

The rider's first job is to stay on the horse at least most of the time.

In my experience, falling off a horse is only occasionally fun. Kids riding piggyback can stay on by pulling the carrier's hair or hold on by strangling their carrier around the neck or chest, but they aren't going to be invited for many piggyback rides that way. Similarly, horses tend not to give their best when being ridden isn't enjoyable for them.

This puts the burden of figuring out how to stay on without causing the horse discomfort exactly where it belongs: on riders.

If you keep the horse between you and the ground, things can't be all that bad. Even if you fell off once or twice every ride, that still means you stayed on for probably thousands of strides. There is always something good to build on! Anything that makes your riding even a smidgen easier and more comfortable for you and the horse is a starting point to continuous improvement. The only trick is to understand better and better what works best for both horse and rider.

The rider's second job is to be the horse's religion or ethics teacher.

If they have anything like a normal upbringing, horses have been taught good horse manners by their dams and herdmates from a very young age. Normal horses do know there are standards of behavior with their fellow creatures.

Some horses take the lead in some circumstances and allow others to take the lead in others, like in any good partnership. Horses teach each other acceptable behavior and what they want their herdmates to do more through subtle and not-so-subtle body language than through verbalizing. Similar issues of communication, leadership, and partnership are in play during our piggyback rides. If a child riding piggyback doesn't communicate what is wanted in a way the carrier can understand easily (or makes demands beyond what the carrier knows is a good idea), the child can't rightly blame the carrier for not doing what the kid wants.

Since horses most naturally use body language to communicate with each other and we are obviously in close physical contact with horses when we ride, it makes sense for people to use that channel of communication with them. Horses certainly do use and learn verbal communications, too. However, when what we say verbally or what we say through sets of signals we have taught the horse conflicts with our more subtle body language, horses tend to believe our body language, often at a remarkably delicate level. Interestingly, many studies confirm that human body language communicates our sense of self at any moment far more accurately than do our words. Even if our body language is subconscious and very subtle indeed, this is exactly the channel of communication horses use routinely. Riding involves attending to this two-way body language at a level we often do not use consciously in our daily activities, but which horses use as a matter of course among themselves.

Still, the burden of explaining the job we want a horse to do in a way it can easily understand and perform lies exactly where it belongs: on riders. Luckily, the same things that make for clear physical communication with a horse also make the horse's job easier to do, as we will see. In fact, you could say that making something easy and enjoyable for a horse to do is exactly the same as telling the horse that's what we want it to do.

Horses must generally be cooperative, peace-seeking creatures. They could stomp each other or us to bits if they wanted to, but that is a rare event even over the course of recorded history. If a thousand-pound animal seriously doesn't intend to do something we want it to do, there is only so much we small humans can do about it without resorting to the many ways we have devised to inflict pain. Aside from showing a lack of creativity and the questionable ethics of inflicting pain just to get our own way, it doesn't make sense, even from a very unsentimental viewpoint, to psychologically or physically damage the horse we want to work for us. I have consistently found that resorting to violence or even discomfort is rarely necessary when people have prepared their horses well for their jobs. Unpleasantness seems to crop up most often when people have not been aware of and dealt with more subtle signs of trouble brewing, signs that any horse would expect another horse to pick up on easily.

The head honcho in a herd doesn't take much flak from the rest of the herd members, so I have no ethical problem with requiring horses to show people at least as much respect as they show their herd leader(s). There are also situations, mostly medical, in which responsible people must physically dominate a horse for its own well-being. Still, inflicting pain on a horse as a first or common resort with any frequency at all is a sure sign that the human is unwise or simply unaware of more sensible ways to establish leadership or to keep high standards of performance. After all, leaders in horse herds rarely have to resort to physical attack to maintain their jurisdiction. I would hope we are at least as smart as our horses in that respect, and observant enough to learn how to get our message across in a way horses can most easily understand.

But unpleasantness is unusual in most barns, so we already have a lot of success to build on to do our second job: keeping in good partnership communication with the horse, with the rider as the majority interest partner who has the right, even the obligation, to set a good standard of performance. Luckily, we must already be pretty good at this, or we would rarely even make it from the field to the barn and on to the arena or trails.

The rider's third job is to be the horse's gym teacher.

Riders will get the most from their horses for the longest period if they have a clear understanding of the gymnastic demands their sport makes on their horse. Coaches who are not as clear on how to develop an athlete physically and mentally as they are about the rules of whatever game is played are likely to have players do things that will be hard on their health and attitude in the long run. I prefer a gym teacher who can help me as an athlete to get a trophy or have fun, whichever I'm after, without damaging my knees and shoulders and back on the way.

Children getting carried piggyback are going to get the most out of their carriers if they ask for the kind of ride the carrier can give at the moment without injury. Even better would be to ask for the kind of a ride that will improve the carrier's overall health and happiness. With lots of rides that gradually strengthen the carrier's weaknesses, both parties can both have more fun and more wins in the long run.

This puts the burden of learning as much as possible about how horses go about the things we ask them to do exactly where it should be: on riders. The second part of this book will give you many approaches and discuss how to tell if what you are doing is working well.

Good riding comes from being in a place from which we can safely and clearly communicate what we want to our horses in a way they can easily understand and easily get their part of the job done. If we are extra smart about our time and money, or if we care about our horses, the jobs we ask horses to do will benefit their mental and physical health at the same time it improves their performance.

As we will find, the same things that make us most secure on our horses also make us clear communicators and reliable leaders for them. A good seat makes for good communication. Understanding how our seat and aids influence the horse—and vice versa—leads to good gymnastic development of the horse and the rider. The end results of a secure seat, clear communication, and wise job assignments are improved performance, health, and even beauty for both horse and rider.

To consider why we may not have learned the easiest way to accomplish these goals so far and how we could learn to accomplish them more easily in the future, lets take a good look at how people learn what we learn.

How We Learn about Anything

Good riding has more to do with what we learn every time we ride than with how well we ride at the moment. So, before we get into *what* to learn about riding, let's consider *how* we learn in general. Learning machines that people are, we can take advantage of our built-in talent to learn much more than we are officially taught.

A fellow by the name of Frank Smith was probably the kind of teacher we all wish we had in school. As far as I can tell, he had nothing to do with horses. But in *The Book of Learning and Forgetting*, he says a lot about learning that applies directly to learning both about how we ride now and how to ride more like we want to ride later. The question here is not whether the standard of performance in the sport you like is better or worse than in any other sport, but how we learn about any riding discipline.

Our friend, Frank, makes three interesting points about learning anything:
- Most of what we learn was never specifically taught;
- You learn primarily what the people you identify with know, whether they mean to teach that or not, and whether you mean to learn that or not; and,
- It is virtually impossible to forget something you didn't learn consciously.

WHAT WE LEARN
Our school days may have led us to believe that teaching and learning are only the transmitting and absorbing of a certain set of facts or experiences or stan-

dards. That overlooks most of what is going on as we learn. The same is true in riding. Frank's first point about learning anything can easily be made by asking a simple question: what do you remember most about school?

You probably remember a lot about what it is like to go to school, about what it is like to take a test, about what it is like to be a student, and so forth. Most of what you remember, what you "know," about your school days has very little to do with facts you were specifically taught in the classroom. It is quite possible you have long forgotten things you were specifically taught, such as the exact dates of important historical events. At the same time, you likely remember whether you liked history class or what you think of folks who do or don't like history. These are all things you were *not* specifically taught.

Very likely, someone can more easily convince you that you might be wrong about some history date you were specifically taught than they could convince you that history and historians are fun, interesting, and useful (or dull, boring, and irrelevant). We are often very certain about things that we were never specifically taught and a little fuzzy about things that we were specifically taught.

We are often surprised to realize we learned something we didn't consciously know we learned; *it is double tough to consciously try to use things we learned unconsciously (if they are "correct") or change them (if they are "wrong").* Things we didn't know we learned can easily become very automatic responses. They can come up so fast we don't really know why we react certain ways sometimes, or even that we are in fact acting differently than we mean to. But somehow we learned to act certain ways, in riding as in anything else.

WHO WE LEARN FROM

People are by nature learning machines. It is virtually impossible to spend five waking minutes doing anything, or even doing nothing, without learning something about what we see, hear, feel, smell, and taste, as well as something about our memories, expectations, and emotions. We are always processing information and experience.

We learn many things much the way children learn to speak from the people around them. Kids brought up by French speakers are not going to pop up speaking Italian out of the blue. Similarly, we wouldn't expect riders who start out riding, say, Saddlebreds, to pick up as much about dressage as someone who grew up around warmbloods. That doesn't mean folks who have studied dressage and folks who have studied gaited horses don't have useful knowledge for each other, perhaps something in the area of precision gait mechanics. Event riders may have more in common with cowboys than they think, too. We can easily miss good information if we do not believe it applies to us or we don't expect to use it personally, whether or not the information is actually true or false or useful.

Much of what we learn unconsciously comes from what people do rather than what they say. You may be taught officially that horses are sensitive creatures, yet commonly see riders pulling hard on reins to make a horse turn or stop or using whips and spurs to get a horse to respond to leg aids. It may be your own experience that the horses you ride are dull and unresponsive. It is very easy to conclude that the horse's sensitivity isn't as refined as you may first have thought the speaker meant, or that the horse you ride is different. You may subtly learn that it is OK to ignore that part of horses' makeup for the sake of getting a particular performance, or that horses are pretty tough characters and respond only to power and force. Asking about the conflict between what is said and what is done may well not yield a clear answer.

LEARNING AND FORGETTING

Learning from whatever is around us is so common that we often don't especially notice how much new information we gather in the course of each day, or how much information we pass over. We tend to think learning only counts if it is done consciously and intentionally. We tend to think things we learn unconsciously or unintentionally don't count or that we don't know them. But much of what we learn, the kinds of things that stick, we learn unintentionally, even unconsciously. Many times, we don't even know we learned something until after it is already well ingrained. We may "know" that foxhunting (or dressage or Western pleasure) is "better" than English pleasure or reining, for example, but that may just be a common view among

Sports we usually think are very different from each other often turn out to have more in common than not.

those we ride with. We may "know" whether we are good at something (pirouettes or jumping or canter leads) or not, when we just haven't understood it very well yet.

We also frequently dismiss the things we do know very well just because we don't have a particular word for them. For example, we may know that there are times when a horse is ready to slide into a lovely canter, without ever having heard the words leads, lateral balance, gait phases, or impulsion. That doesn't mean we don't know about them. We have to file our knowledge under some more general and often more emotional category, like "good" or "more fun" or "wonderful." Learning more specifically what made it wonderful will make your experience easier to talk about, but lacking jargon (or the latest catch-phrase) doesn't mean we don't have useable knowledge.

At least some of what we learn so effectively, we would prefer not to have learned or would like to forget, but seem unable to do so. This is true in riding, just like in anything else. For example, we all have certain words that we usually misspell, and we usually misspell them the same way. It's not that we didn't learn to spell a word; rather, we learned very well to spell it incorrectly. What we learn first tends to stick with us, even when we would like to learn a better way of doing something later on. Similarly, riders who start learning to jump by standing in the stirrups many strides before a small jump can find it almost impossible to resist creeping up the horse's neck while approaching a fence on a horse who requires more guidance.

As we will see, there are apparently quite a few natural reasons for hanging on to the first way we learn to do things, even if that is not what we will finally want to do. Not absorbing information fully and accurately are other ways we could misinterpret what is going on around us and therefore block our best response. It is easy to stick with something that seems close enough, but isn't actually well considered.

We are continuously processing and learning, including learning how to routinely ignore much of what goes on within and around us. For the most part, that's fine. Our brains senses every moment whether or not the chair we are sitting on is steady; we don't need to pay attention to that unless it changes. But it is a good idea to pay attention to the small squeaks that come before the chair does suddenly break. We can be surprised even though there were signs something was likely to go wrong.

Jumping to conclusions—acting on partial information—is another way we could "know" things that aren't entirely true. Humans may have a built-in tendency to react quickly to partial information. One theory says that early humans were more likely to survive if they ran when the bushes rustled, rather than waiting to find out if it was a tiger or a rabbit shaking the leaves. That kind of reaction is not necessarily bad, but it can be tiring. The folks who ran fast but also got fast at telling whether it was a tiger or a rabbit rustling the bushes had more time to discuss their dinner plans, perhaps including the rabbit.

INSTRUCTION AND LEARNING

We can and do learn easily, but we are not always aware of what we are learning. What we learn is not necessarily what we are going to remember and use most easily. What we learn does not automatically include everything that is true or useful.

What has this all got to do with riding? Everything.

Let me ask you a few questions about what you know about riding.

Is one breed better than another? Is one gait or transition more difficult than another? Is it easier to sit a slow trot than an extended trot? Is jumping more dangerous than trail riding? Are Western riders better than English riders? Is telling what lead a horse is on without looking only something for pretty advanced riders?

We all have answers for these questions, but they are not necessarily facts. Only one of these questions can be answered with a measurable statistic: trail riding is statistically far more dangerous than jumping . . . and catching and grooming a horse is more dangerous than either of those!

It is worth the effort to obtain facts before we form fixed opinions, even though that may not be mankind's built-in first tendency. The conclusions we draw will be much more useful for the effort. This has certain challenges, since we may honestly not realize we are operating on opinions and partial information rather than facts.

What we have learned but don't know we have learned can be very compelling. It can make a difference in what we actually do versus what we mean to do. This is just as true for Olympic-level riders as for students trying their first trot strides.

Outside instructions and self-given instructions can be right on target. Yet, we don't always follow instructions even if we really mean to follow them. As common and perhaps natural as this is, there is always a way to change a vicious cycle into a virtuous one. Very often, the change that makes a difference is so simple or subtle we just overlooked it. We may not want to "waste time" if it seems contrary to something we "know," or does not seem to apply to the sport we like. What ends up working may well seem at first too easy to make much difference in something that looks difficult.

WHERE WE ARE AT THE MOMENT AND WHERE WE WANT TO END UP

We probably all have a sense that some things about our riding could be better, and that some things are getting pretty good. We may think of this as riding a particular course or routine or getting to a certain competition. We have a certain mental picture of what that would be like. Goals certainly influence how we go about things. But "getting it right" isn't always as clear a directive as it seems.

There are plenty of descriptions or demonstrations of the "right" way to do anything in riding, but they don't always agree, even within the same sport. As soon as we learn something that is supposedly written in stone, we can easily find a rider who doesn't ride that way, gets good results anyway, and has very plausible reasons for doing what they do. What works for us personally also changes over time. Our goals sometimes seem as changeable as clouds against a clear blue sky.

How can we possibly decide what will get us where we want to go?

There is another question we must ask before we decide what is "right."

We can't decide if our heels or hands or head are in the right place or the wrong place if we don't know where they are in the first place. We've all

The first time I fell off was the first time I was being taught to canter. The horse (whose name and markings I still remember over 30 years later) went into one of those really awkward trots before he cantered, and I was simply jostled off Notorious' copper chestnut back and got a close-up look at his three stockings. What I learned at some level from that one experience was that cantering is hard to do and that I wasn't good at it anyway. I eventually began to think maybe I wasn't even a good rider, and maybe I never would be, since I saw other people had no problem getting Notorious to canter and staying on, too. Not surprisingly, I spent over a year not being able to get any horse to canter, which seemed to confirm what I "knew" about cantering and my riding ability. I soon lost my initial fear of trying to canter, since the chances of it happening seemed remote anyway. So, fear of falling off at the canter wasn't exactly the problem. Although at eight or nine years old, I may not have been able to express all this well, that doesn't mean I didn't "know" it.

Eventually, some horse did canter for me "by mistake." I didn't know the horse was cantering, just that it was doing something different and quite wonderful. It wasn't until I'd done that quite a few times that someone told me the horse was cantering. Aside from the interesting question of how I had gotten the horse to canter repeatedly without having "learned" the aids to canter, I realized I had been working with a rather incomplete idea about cantering and my cantering ability and horses' willingness to canter and what it would be like if they did and so forth. My idea of what belonged with the word "canter" expanded considerably after I experienced it without specifically being taught. I also realized I had never actually had the experience of cantering, since I had fallen off before the horse got to that—not that that had stopped me from having all sorts of rather jumbled and persistent problems with cantering for so long. I had also missed out for a year on my suddenly favorite thing to do.

How long did it take to fix the problem? A year . . . or one experience unclouded by misperceptions?

experienced this, both on horseback and off. One minute we know our heels or hands are just fine. The next moment they aren't on the radar screen.

We may know more about where we want to end up as riders than we know about our riding from moment to moment. But getting from where you are (point A) to where you want to be (point B) is harder when you don't know where both A and B are. What *should* be can easily overshadow what simply *is*!

We are often unaware of how our bodies do the things we do. For example, much of our body language, such as facial expression and gestures, is quite unconscious. That's mostly OK, but unconscious action does leave a wide-open area for riding in ways that we didn't know we learned. These must be mostly good ways, or we would fall off more than we stay on, frequently go left when we meant to right, and break our horses down constantly.

For a lot of perfectly valid reasons, sometimes just by our physical design and sometimes because of things we learned without knowing we learned them, it is remarkably easy to judge that something about our riding is right or wrong or better or worse without actually knowing what we are talking about.

A judgment is different than an observation. A judgment indicates whether we like something better than something else. A judgment can depend on our mood or our past experience or our expectations and may very well come from many things we didn't know we learned. Judgments often confirm what we already believe is true.

On the other hand, an observation can be measured. Accurate observation depends on our ability to objectively sense what is happening. Observation deals with facts and often leads to new information. I find that getting better at knowing what is happening is the key to getting better at what we want to happen, in riding perhaps more than any other sport.

Riders often have to sort out why horses do the things they do. Horses can take our communications very literally, like a person who turns left when we say to turn left. But they can also take what we meant to say into account, like a person who turns left when we mistakenly say to turn right. How that happens is an interesting question, but we have all experienced it. If we aren't very clear on what we are doing as riders and therefore how the horse experiences us as riders, we can't possibly figure out the most basic question of whether a horse did something because we told them to, or for some other reason. That basic decision is the starting point for all of our interactions with horses, so riders need to stay 100 percent clear about how the horse experiences us as riders. Accurate observation will serve that better than opinions.

Even if we are not naturally 100 percent aware of everything we do as we ride, we can be sure our horses know all about it. They feel everything riders do, just as you would if you were in their position. What they decide to do about what they feel riders do is a slightly different question. But we must consider how the horse experiences our riding before we can fairly judge the horse's responses. Ultimately, only our own personal sensory systems can tell us what we actually are doing and, therefore, how another creature understands our actions. That makes a high level of sensitivity to ourselves and another living creature prime requirements for good riding. No wonder riding is said to be very character-building!

THE IDEAL RIDE

It helps a lot to keep the ideal ride in mind, although even the best riders don't achieve that all the time. Even the highest level rider—perhaps especially the highest level riders—are well aware that they are not always riding at their own personal best.

Horses that are ridden well more often than not will frequently make up for our mistakes, just like a good dance partner can help you through a bad step or two. Horses that rarely experience being well-ridden have a hard time learning what we would like to happen and little incentive to help us get the job done when we aren't riding perfectly.

Learning about what gets in the way and also what promotes our ever-changing personal best allows our personal best to show up more often. It seems to me that is all horses require of us as riders. Thinking that constant ideal riding is the only acceptable level of performance can easily lead to learning more about what we are doing "wrong" than what we are doing "right." Knowing a lot about what is "wrong" about ourselves and our horses (and other

THE SEAMLESS SEAT

CHAPTER 1

Finding Your Own Personal Ideal Seat

I enjoy surprising myself.
—Peter Ustinov

I act, and by my actions learn who I am.
—Descartes

In every riding sport, a good seat uses the horse's movements to the rider's advantage, so more movement from the horse makes for an even better seat.

A good seat will be:

- secure, for safety, so we don't make decisions out of unnecessary fear;
- comfortable, sustainable, and healthy, without concussion or friction or strain; and,
- effective, getting the most results for least effort, so we can do more fun things with our horses.

A good seat works with the laws of Nature, since it is pointless to fight them. A good seat makes it easier for the horse to work and easier for the horse to understand our aids. The ultimate test of your seat is that the horse's performance improves and its mental and physical well-being are at least maintained and, preferably, improved.

First, we need to find out where your seat is at present. So we'll start with a thorough inventory of your seat. Then we'll think about how to move from where you are to the ideal seat for you, in your sport, on your horse.

To discuss this, we need to agree on some definitions.

THE PLATFORM AND CONTACT AREA

We are going to call the parts of our pelvis that connect with the horse our *platform*. The platform is made up of your two seatbones and the area in front of the seatbones, which for politeness' sake we will call the area in front of the seatbones. This is the base of your pelvis, the area between your two hip joint sockets at the very tops of your thighs. The base of your pelvis is what your upper body rests on in the saddle and where your legs hang from, so it will influence everything else about your riding. Bareback or saddled, your platform is also what the horse experiences most directly about you as a rider.

Please take a moment to locate your hip joints: they are at the top of your thighbones. Stand up and swing your whole leg back and forth a bit to help locate where your thigh bones connect with your pelvis. It's lower than most people think it is. Next, sit down for a moment and locate your two seatbones. If you move around a bit on your seatbones, you will see that it doesn't take much movement to change how your platform connects with the chair. Move your pelvis a bit in various directions, and you will see that your platform orientation makes a big difference especially in how your vertebrae line up and how your upper body and legs are arranged in relation to each other.

We are going to call the parts below our platform our *contact area*. Our contact area runs from the inside top of our thighbones down the inside of our thighs to that knobby bone in the inside of our knees, and perhaps just below the knee and somewhat farther down the inside of our calves. Our contact area may be in contact with the horse via the saddle or directly with the horse as far down as an area somewhere around the inside surface of our knees, or it may run all the way down to our ankles. The exact area depends on the saddle, the rider's length of leg, and the horse's size and build. Contact between some area of our thighbones and the horse is required, preferably as close to the knee as possible, given your build, your horse's build, and your saddle. Please notice I said "contact the horse," not "put the horse's ribcage in a death grip."

Contact with the horse or saddle below the knobby point on the inside of our knee (the lower end of the thighbone) is optional except for jockeys.

Jockeys connect with the horse much lower down their leg, at times only around their ankles and feet, although in much the same place on the horse as other riders connect with the horse with their thighs.

FINDING YOUR SEAT AT THE HALT

You need a horse for this experiment, saddled and bridled. The more likely the horse is just to stand and fall asleep, the better. If your horse is standing slack-hipped, ask it to use all four feet. It doesn't have to stand perfectly squarely, just four-footed.

It would be handy to have a large mirror available. An observer/note-taker will be very useful. Your observer doesn't need to know anything about horses or riding. It may be better if they don't. Some painter's masking tape, the kind that comes off easily, and a camera, especially one that can take instant snapshots, would be great. Video tape is good for reviewing later.

I have provided some Seat Inventory Sheets for you to use. You can copy these pages and take them to the barn with you to have a seat inventory party with your riding buddies. You can also retake your seat inventory now and then to see how things are changing.

These tools offer some ways to track our discoveries in these experiments and others to follow, but all you absolutely need is the tacked-up horse and your own sensory system. "The skin is faster than the eye," as horse and dog trainer Vicki Hearne says in her fine book, *Calling Animals by Name*. All of these experiments are just to get your sensory system more alive and accurate.

First, we'll locate your platform in the saddle. Sit in the saddle as usual, with both feet in the stirrups, and note the points on the first Seat Inventory Sheet, Locating Your Platform, page 6.

There isn't much but skin between our seatbones and the saddle unless we roll back toward our tailbone or squeeze what we will politely call our tushie muscles. Check out where along your seatbones and the area in front of your seatbone you feel the most connection with the saddle. Check out how those points of connection with the saddle or horse change if you move around. Even small movements like tipping your head, clenching your stom-ach muscles, pushing your toes down, holding an elbow away from your side, or tipping your head or shoulders various ways could change how your upper body's weight falls through your platform onto the saddle. Now you know how to find your platform in the saddle. You also have a sense of how much movement it takes to change what the horse experiences about you as a rider.

If you see or feel something you think is "wrong" as you make these observations, please don't try to fix it forever just yet. It is just as useful to get a sense of something "wrong" as of something "right." We may also end up deciding something isn't as wrong or as right as we thought.

Next, we'll locate your contact area. Use your second Seat Inventory Sheet, Locating Your Contact Area, page 7.

Notice where along the length of each leg you feel contact with the sad-dle or the horse. Take it inch by inch, one leg at a time, and then get a feel for the whole area of contact on each side of the horse. You can run your fingers along the edges of your leg connections with the saddle or the horse, as if you were tracing the outline of your contact area. You can have your observer run a finger along the outline of the areas you can't reach, to help you become more sensitive to your contact area with the horse.

Imagine you slathered colored ink all over your inseams before you mounted up. What areas on the saddle and horse would pick up an ink stain? Notice that the outline of such an ink stain isn't necessarily the same as the outline of your leg that you could trace on a photograph. It may also not be the same on the left side and the right side.

Next, we will look at how your platform and contact area relate to each other, starting with the third Seat Inventory Sheet, From the Left Side, page 7.

Move your horse over to the mirror if you have one available, so that you can look at your left side. Make mental notes of the points of interest on your third Seat Inventory Sheet, From the Left Side, and have your observer make notes or draw or take a picture. You can mark points of interest with masking tape on your tack and horse if your horse is OK with that. Then, make the same personal observations, notes, drawings, marks, or photos for your right side as you did for the left. Use your fourth Seat Inventory Sheet, From the

Right Side, page 8, for that. They may well be quite different than what you observed on the left side.

Next, turn your horse to face the mirror if you are using one, or have your observer move around to the front of the horse. There's another Seat Inventory Sheet for you to use, From the Front, page 9. Note/draw/photograph/video/ mark with tape these points of interest. Then, have your observer move directly behind the horse and note the points of interest on the Seat Inventory Sheet, From the Back, page 11. If your horse is OK with it, you can even use a long carpenter's level to find out if your hips, ribcage, shoulders, and ears are level. This isn't a view riders often use to evaluate their seat, but it can be very telling indeed and often points to why other seat problems have not been easy to fix.

You now have quite a complete inventory of your physical arrangement on the horse for the moment. We don't know what is "good" or "bad" yet. We only know where your platform and contact area are for the moment. This could easily change if your horse moves around, if you change horses or saddles, or

How your platform supports your spine changes your contact area and what the horse must do to support you.

repeat the inventory half an hour later, or when the weather is warmer or colder, or you are better rested, etc. No problem. It's just some information to start with. Please try to avoid the tendency to decide something is right or wrong and jump to fix it at this point. You are invited, though, to take time to become more sensitive about how your parts feel in relation to each other and how they connect to the horse.

If you are like most people, you discovered some asymmetries in how you are arranged on the horse that you didn't know about before. If you ride around a bit and then repeat the inventory a few times, you will also know that they are not fixed in stone. You may be speculating about how those asymmetries influence your riding. More important is that you have taken the time to accurately observe how you are arranged on the horse. Simple observation is an important step to take *before* you start making judgments.

Seat Inventory Sheet 1: Locating Your Platform	
Check this out	Notes
Notice how your weight falls into the saddle.	
Where along the length of your seatbones is the most weight, the clearest connection with the saddle?	
How is your weight distributed over your seatbones and area in front of your seatbone? More on the area in front of your seatbone? More on your seatbones? More on one side than the other?	
On what spot in the saddle do they connect?	

Seat Inventory Sheet 2: Locating Your Contact Area

Check this out	Notes
What parts of your saddle and horse would pick up an ink stain from your clothes?	
What areas wouldn't get any ink on them?	
What would the outline of the ink stain be?	
Would the ink stain be the same on the left side as the right?	
If the ink got brighter if it was pressed on more firmly, what areas of the ink stain would be brighter?	
If this wonderful ink could seep through your skin and muscles, what areas on your leg bones would be stained, and how brightly?	

Seat Inventory Sheet 3: From the Left Side

Check this out	Notes
Where is your shoulder in relation to your hip?	
Where is your ear in relation to your shoulder?	

Seat Inventory Sheet 3: From the Left Side (*cont.*)

How much space is there between your tushie and the back edge of the cantle?	
At what angle is your thigh?	
At what point on the saddle does your knee lie?	
Where is your stirrup in relation to the girth?	
Where along the sole of your foot does the stirrup lie?	
Does your foot lie more to the inside or outside of the stirrup?	
What is the angle between your shin and the top of your foot?	

Seat Inventory Sheet 4: From the Right Side

Check this out	Notes
Where is your shoulder in relation to your hip?	
Where is your ear in relation to your shoulder?	
How much space is there between your tushie and the back edge of the cantle?	

Seat Inventory Sheet 4: From the Right Side (*cont.*)

At what angle is your thigh?	
At what point on the saddle does your knee lie?	
Where is your stirrup in relation to the girth?	
Where along the sole of your foot does the stirrup lie?	
Does your foot lie more to the inside or outside of the stirrup?	
What is the angle between your shin and the top of your foot?	

Seat Inventory Sheet 5: From the Front

Check this out	Notes
Where is your left foot pointing?	
Where is your right foot pointing?	
Are they pointing equally toward or away from the horse?	
Is the outside or the inside of your left foot more in contact with the stirrup, or is it flat across the stirrup?	

Seat Inventory Sheet 5: From the Front (*cont.*)	
Is the outside or the inside of your right foot more in contact with the stirrup, or is it flat across the stirrup?	
Can you see more of the top of your boot or the sole of your boot on each foot?	
Where are your toes in relation to your ankles on each foot?	
Moving upward, what part of your left calf is in contact with the horse or saddle?	
What part of your right calf is in contact with the horse or saddle?	
Are your knees pointing equally toward or away from the horse?	
Are your knees even with each other, or is one higher than the other?	
When the horse is looking straight ahead, do its ears cover the same place on the left and right sides of your belly or chest?	
If you drew a line straight upward from each of the horse's ears (if the horse is looking straight ahead), would your upper body be closer to one line than the other?	

Seat Inventory Sheet 5: From the Front (*cont.*)

If you are wearing a shirt with buttons down the middle, or a pattern with vertical lines, how do the buttons or lines line up?	
Are your hips level?	
If you are wearing a belt or have your shirt tucked in, is the belt or the waistline of your breeches level?	
Is your ribcage level?	
Are your shoulders level?	
If you are wearing a shirt with a horizontal pattern, how do the lines line up?	
Stick a finger in each ear. Are your ears level?	
If you had a long antenna attached to the top of your hat, where would it point?	

Seat Inventory Sheet 6: From the Back

Check this out	Notes
Where is your left foot pointing?	
Where is your right foot pointing?	

Seat Inventory Sheet 6: From the Back (*cont.*)

Are your toes pointing equally toward or away from the horse?	
Where are your toes in relation to your ankles on the left side?	
Where are your toes in relation to your ankles on the right side?	
Moving upward, what part of your left calf is in contact with the horse or saddle?	
What part of your right calf is in contact with the horse or saddle?	
Are your knees pointing equally toward or away from the horse?	
Are your knees even with each other? Is one higher than the other?	
Is the gullet of the saddle square over the horse's spine?	
When the horse is looking straight ahead, how is your spine oriented to the horse's spine?	
If you drew a line straight upward from each of the horse's hind legs, would your upper body be closer to one line than the other?	

Seat Inventory Sheet 6: From the Back (*cont.*)	
If the horse's tail is hanging straight down, drawn an imaginary line straight up. How would your spine be aligned with that line?	
If your pants have a seam in the middle, how is that lined up with the horse's spine?	
Are your hips level?	
If you are wearing a belt or have your shirt tucked in, is the belt or the waistline level?	
Are your shoulders level?	
If you are wearing a shirt with a horizontal pattern, how do the lines line up?	
Are your ears level?	
If you had a long antenna attached to the top of your hat where would it point?	

How the Platform and the Contact Area Work with Each Other

How our platform is arranged greatly influences our contact area. Our platform is flexibly connected to the tops of our thighs by ligaments, tendons, and muscles around our hip joints. How our pelvis and therefore hip joints

Same upper body inclination in each of these three photos, but very different arrangements between the riders' platform and contact areas. Notice how differently each rider's weight is arranged on the horse and in the stirrups. Their platform/contact area arrangement makes more difference than how far forward the rider leans.

are oriented has a lot to do with how our spine is supported and how the rest of our leg will connect with the horse. We can tip our pelvis back and forth or from side to side somewhat without changing our thighs, knees, or ankles, but not very far. You can turn your lower leg in or out without changing how your thigh rotates in your hip joints, but, again, not very far.

Your platform orientation makes a big difference in how your weight travels to the ground, or if you are riding, how it travels to your stirrups. Your platform orientation makes a big difference in which muscles you will have to use in the rest of your leg to have it move certain ways, how the joints operate, and how your whole leg is oriented toward the horse. Since our legs support us in riding as well as off the horse, how our pelvis and legs relate to each other is basic to how we operate.

Your platform orientation also makes a big difference in how your spine is supported and how it operates. The tops of our thighs are connected to our lower back by the internal psoas muscles that run from the top of each thigh-bone through the pelvis to the front of each lumbar vertebra. Your platform arrangement will certainly influence how the psoas muscles connect your torso with your legs, so it has a lot to do with how our lower back and legs coordinate. If you are having problems with either your upper body or your contact area, check how another platform arrangement might make things easier. Other than anything obviously unsafe, like hooking spurs into the horse's sides, try new arrangements out *before* you decide they are wrong. They might not turn out to be as wrong as you thought, and they might provide some useful information anyway.

Changes in your platform are going to show up in everything from toes to head. Our horses know all about our platform/contact area/upper body relationship, just as we would if we were in their position: on the receiving end of how we have arranged ourselves over their backs and along their sides.

Our platform and contact area are physically interconnected, but other things also influence our platform and contact area relationship.

Our legs will hang differently out of our hip joints on a wider horse than on a narrower one, and a smaller horse is going to offer a different contact area and carry our legs differently than a tall one. Some riders are physically more comfortable on wider horses, some riders are more comfortable on narrower horses.

A saddle can either help a rider tremendously or greatly complicate learning to ride well. As the saying goes, you have to be either a very good rider or a very poor one, not to be influenced by the saddle you are using. Saddles can make a big difference in how easily your platform supports your spine, whether it is easy for you to coordinate your contact area with your platform, and where your weight lies on the horse's back. Riders in saddles that don't fit them are constantly working against the alignment and balance the saddles give them. That's an unfortunate start to things. Just because you have gotten used to a saddle doesn't mean it is the best one for you.

Different sports also require different ranges of motion for the rider to agree with the changes in the horse's center of gravity, so it makes sense that our platform/contact area relationships vary among the horse sports, too. A

Eventing! A wider base of support (more horizontal thigh, more knee angle, shorter stirrups) is useful for the wide range of demands on a cross-country course.

A narrower base of support (more vertical thigh, less bend at the knee, longer stiruups), but notice that the rider's weight is still quite close to the horse's shoulders.

wider base of support allows more latitude for your center of gravity to move around and still be within your base of support. The more horizontal your thigh is, the wider your base of support. It will be easier to move your upper body from vertical to forward by flexing at the hip joint when your thigh is more horizontal. So, if your sport might require wide variations in your center of gravity, like jumping big fences out of a collected canter, a wider base of support is a good idea. In riding terms, this means a shorter stirrup and more bend in the knees.

Dressage riders and Western pleasure horse riders, for example, are less likely to need the very wide range of changes in their center of gravity than jump riders need. They can trade the narrower base of support for the advantage of the greater contact area possible with a more vertical leg. As we will see, this hopefully does not mean getting lighter in the stirrups or heavy on the horse's back.

So, the "right" contact area is not fixed in stone by any means. There is no single platform or contact area arrangement that will suit everyone all the time. Look at any group of successful riders and you will see that riders may well change from one platform orientation to another, sometimes quite rapidly, sometimes gradually, sometimes for a moment, sometimes for quite some time. Just as platform orientations change, riders may well change from one contact area to another. The question isn't which platform and contact area is right, but which platform and contact area you have at the moment and how that is working for you on this horse, for this stride.

Finding Your Easiest Lineup

Here's a simple way to find the body arrangement that allows your skeleton its finest balance and freedom of motion. Then we can consider how to use our new observations in action.

Before we do this experiment, we have to make sure your stirrups are even. You should do this periodically anyway, since leather stretches, and what

Three partners at the same task: How does each rider's platform/contact area arrangement influence their horse?

used to be an even adjustment gradually becomes uneven. Do not rely on counting what holes you have adjusted your stirrup leathers to.

For Western saddles, you will have to unsaddle the horse and find a place to hang the saddle, like on a saddle rack or a fence, and you will need a carpenter's level. Put the saddle on the rack or the fence, and adjust it so the skirts are level. Run a broom handle through both stirrups and check if the broomstick is level. Adjust the stirrups so the skirts and the stirrups are both dead level.

For English saddles, you can strip the stirrups off the saddle by slipping the still-buckled stirrup leather backward off the stirrup bar. Hang the stirrup leathers over your outstretched hand with the buckles near your hand. If your stirrups are offset, rotate one leather and stirrup around so they are both angled the same way. Check to see if the bottoms of the stirrups are even with each other. Adjust them and reattach them to the saddle.

Saddle up again and remount. If you need to adjust the length of your stirrups, make sure you adjust both of them the same amount, even is that feels odd at the moment. Make sure the saddle is square on the horse by lining the pommel up with the horse's withers.

Get your horse lined up with a mirror so your can see your left side, or have your observer ready to make notes about/draw/photograph your left side. Try this:

Grab a bit of mane and stand tall in your stirrups, up on your toes, ballerina-style, straight-legged. Lots of things probably just happened. How easily did you rise from the saddle? Did you have to change where your foot is in one stirrup, or in both, to do this?

Notice that all it took to be very far away from the saddle with a very narrow base of support was to activate the muscles that push our toes down and straighten our knees and hips.

This is not a very stable arrangement, especially if your hips are hanging out behind your legs, so please hold a bit of the horse's mane so you can soften your landing on the horse's back if you lose your balance.

Let's start our observations on the left side, and start from the bottom. Use the On Your Toes Inventory Sheet 1: From the Left Side, facing page, to note your observations. Check the right side, using On Your Toes Inventory Sheet 2: From the Right Side, page 22, looking at the same points of interest.

If you compare these notes with the ones you made earlier when you were seated, chances are that these points are much more closely lined up vertically than they were when you were sitting in the saddle. Our bodies do know how to line up well vertically. And it doesn't take much leg muscle to push ourselves very far away from the horse.

Now, move so you can see yourself in the mirror from the front, or have your observer move to the front, and note/draw/photograph/mark the points of interest on the On-Your-Toes Inventory Sheet 3: From the Front, page 22. Then, have your observer move behind you, and let's take a look, using the On-Your-Toes Inventory Sheet 4: From the Back, page 24.

On-Your-Toes Inventory Sheet 1: From the Left Side	
Check this out	Notes
Where is your left stirrup in relation to the girth?	
Where is your lower left leg in relation to the girth? Is that different from where it was when you were sitting in the saddle?	
Where is your left knee in relation to the girth?	
Where is your left shoulder in relation to your left hip joint?	
Where is your imaginary antenna pointing now?	

On-Your-Toes Inventory Sheet 2: From the Right Side

Check this out	Notes
Where is your right stirrup in relation to the girth now?	
Where is your lower right leg in relation to the girth? Is that different than where it was when you were sitting in the saddle?	
Where is your right knee in relation to the girth?	
Where is your right shoulder in relation to your right hip joint?	
Where is your imaginary antenna pointing now?	

On-Your-Toes Inventory Sheet 3: From the Front

Check this out	Notes
How are your feet placed in the stirrups?	
Are they pointing in or out the same way they were when you were sitting?	
Is one pointing in or out more than the other?	
Are both feet contacting the stirrups the same way?	

On-Your-Toes Inventory Sheet 3: From the Front (*cont.*)	
Where is your weight across the stirrup? Across the middle, to the inside or the outside?	
Is that the same in both stirrups?	
How are your ankles placed in relation to your toes? Are they more to the inside or outside of your toes?	
Is that ankle/toe arrangement the same on both sides?	
Moving upward, is your lower left leg angled away from the horse differently than your right lower leg?	
Are your knees level with each other?	
Is one knee pointed more in or out than the other?	
Is your kneecap closer to the saddle on one side than the other?	
If you drew a line from one front hip bone to the other, would it be level?	
If you extended that line outward to both sides, would it point directly left and right of the horse, or would one side be pointing more backward or forward?	
Are your hips off to one side?	

On-Your-Toes Inventory Sheet 3: From the Front (*cont.*)	
Where is your left shoulder in relation to your left hip joint?	
Where is your right shoulder in relation to your right hip joint?	
Are your shoulders level?	
Are they square above your hips?	
If you drew a line down your sternum (the bony line where the two sides of your rib cage join), where would it point?	
Where is your imaginary antenna pointing?	

On-Your-Toes Inventory Sheet 4: From the Back	
Check this out	Notes
Is the gullet of the saddle square over the horse's spine?	
When the horse is looking straight ahead, how is your spine oriented to the horse's spine?	
If you drew a line straight upward from each of the horse's hindlegs, would your upper body be closer to one line than the other?	

On-Your-Toes Inventory Sheet 4: From the Back (*cont.*)	
If the horse's tail is hanging straight down, draw an imaginary line straight up. How is your spine aligned with that line?	
If your pants have a seam in the middle, how is that lined up with the horse's spine?	
Are your hips level?	
If you are wearing a belt or have your shirt tucked in, is the belt or the waistline of your pants level?	
Are your shoulders level? If you are wearing a shirt with a horizontal pattern, how do the lines line up?	
Are your ears level?	
If you had a long antenna attached to the top of your hat, where would it point?	

You can sit down now. Gently, please.

You can try this up-on-your-toes experiment a few more times and see how things change or stay the same as you repeat this experiment. Keep in mind the idea isn't to get things right, but just to practice becoming more aware of how you are arranged. We'll get to fixing things if necessary in a bit, but you can't fix anything until you feel it.

You know now that your body is most at ease with your legs (your base of support) under your center of gravity (somewhere in the lower third of your torso, most likely), or perhaps even a bit behind it. If you are not aligned with gravity, your body will automatically seek outside support by gripping the saddle, pushing on stirrups, pulling on the mane, or dropping into the saddle. You have found out how your weight transmits to your stirrups when your seat is out of the saddle. You also found out what muscles push you away from the horse.

Let's see what happens when you don't use those muscles.

HEEL RELEASE

It might be a good idea to have your observer read this section to you as you try these experiments. Lift out of the saddle again, up on your toes, ballerina-style. Notice which muscles in your lower leg push you up and hold you up. Don't aim to sit in the saddle yet, but slowly, gently, taking all the time in the world, let your lower leg muscles relax, especially around your ankles and in your calves. Let your own body weight slide down the horse's sides. Let your knees slide down the saddle, too. The stirrups are there to catch your weight, just like the ground catches your weight when you are standing. Hang there in the stirrups awhile. Some arrangement will let your weight drop into the stirrups the most. Don't push. Just hang.

After you let your weight hang into your heels, this, that, and the other muscle will release, and you will slip closer to the saddle thread by thread if you give it time. The point is not to get into the saddle, nor to push your heels low. We just want to find out what happens when you release the muscles in your lower leg, the muscles you were using to push yourself away from the horse and hold you away from it.

As you let your weight slide down the saddle to the stirrups, you may find your ankles get uncomfortable, or something else cramps. If so, lift up again, and let your weight down even more gently, letting your ankles adjust to make everything more and more comfortable. Don't be satisfied with an arrangement you figure you can tolerate. Your ankles have to be positively comfortable. You may want to adjust how your feet lie across one or both stirrups and whether your ankle is more to the inside or the outside of your foot. You might be surprised what changes all the way up your leg and even through your torso and your head might be involved in making your ankles 110 percent comfortable.

"Heels down" is not the point of this exercise, so don't push on your stirrups to try to drive your heels lower. But if you did that, notice what happened to your knees and your hips, how much closer or farther away from the saddle that put you, how it changes where the stirrups are in relation to the girth, and so on.

You don't have to push on your stirrups to have your full weight in them any more than you need to push on the ground when you are standing. For now, just check out how your skeleton hangs into your stirrups as fewer and fewer muscles interfere with letting your whole skeleton line up with gravity. Just let gravity slide your leg down the horse's sides into comfortable, springy ankles, with the stirrups catching your weight.

Have your observer make notes about where the stirrup is in relation to the girth, and what the angle is between your shinbones and the tops of the foot of your boots. See if your observer can tug the stirrup out from under your foot. If they can do that easily at all, your weight isn't in the stirrup. What would be holding your weight away from the stirrup? If you are gripping the saddle with your thighs or knees, your legs can't slip down as far as they otherwise would and your weight won't get fully to the stirrups. If the area in front of your seatbone is already in contact with the saddle, your stirrups may be too long to be able to catch your weight.

What happens to your thigh orientation if you relax muscles high on the inside of your thighs, or across the front of your belly? What happens to your knee contact if you let your kneecaps roll in toward the saddle, as if you were trying to point them toward each other? How does that change your contact area? What changes does that suggest for your platform and upper body? What happens if you let your kneecaps roll outward so the back of your thighs and calves are more in touch with the horse's sides? How does that change things for your platform? What other changes from your platform up to your ears make rolling your knees in or out easier? What if you let your lower leg closer or farther away from the horse? How do all these changes influence how your weight reaches your stirrups? How do they influence your torso, shoulders, neck, and head?

Do you feel more stable and secure when you let your weight drop into the stirrups through relaxed ankle joints than when you push yourself away from the horse by straightening your legs and pushing your toes down?

No doubt you have more new observations. Please make mental notes, or have your observer jot them down, draw them, or take photos.

You can sit down now. Gently, please, gently.

You can repeat this heel release experiment as often as you like, trying this and that arrangement. You may find certain experiments are more or less comfortable and stable. But please remember that we are only making observations, not trying to fix anything yet. Within the limits of safety, you are welcome to try things that you think might turn out wrong. Getting a feel for "wrong" things can help you decide if they really would be wrong under all circumstances or might be useful at times. It sharpens your sense of what is "right," too. The only thing that counts at the moment is finding out what makes you totally comfortable when you let your own body weight hang into the stirrups by releasing your lower leg muscles and orienting your contact area and platform most comfortably.

What do we know now that we didn't know before?

Quite a bit! You no doubt have more observations yourself, but here are a few things to make note of, too.

Notice how much changed just by releasing the muscles that operate one joint in each leg: our ankles. Giving that one joint in each leg free play brought us much closer to the horse, maybe even with the area in front of our seatbone touching the saddle. We also discovered that our ankles will easily accept our weight and transmit it to the stirrups when they are free to move around however our particular ankles are built to move. That can look quite different for one rider than for another and different for the same rider at one time than another.

Notice that it isn't necessary to push our weight forcefully into the stirrup. Dropping our weight into the stirrup by using *fewer* muscles in our lower leg secures us quite effectively.

We can find out even more by taking the same experiment a step further.

KNEE AND HIP RELEASE

Let's see what happens when we also use fewer muscles around our knees and hips, so we gain freedom of motion rather than pitting one set of muscles against another in those areas, too.

Grab a bit of mane again and lift yourself out of the saddle, up on your toes, ballerina-style again. Slowly, gently, taking all the time in the world, let your lower leg muscles relax, just like in the heel release experiment. Let your weight hang freely into the stirrups by letting your ankles drop as far and in whatever foot orientation is easiest and most comfortable for you.

Then, and only then, let your knees slide down and forward as you also allow your tummy to drop toward the horse's withers and let your tushie slide backwards, so the angle between your upper body and your thighs closes. Always looking for any way small or large to be more comfortable, always looking for another muscle fiber to relax, just let your weight hang into your stirrups while your knees slip toward your toes and the horse and your platform slides backwards toward the cantle. It doesn't have to get fully in the saddle yet.

Roll your kneecaps in toward the saddle and out away from it, to see what is easiest. Draw your heels closer to the horse, and then let them away from the horse. How does that influence your knee release? Every saddle has a spot that lets your knee slip into place like a key fits a lock; hopefully that is a place your knees can get to easily, which is to say the saddle fits you. Let things slip around and look for that sweet spot, or for anything that feels more like that. You can try various stirrup lengths to see which lets your knee cozy down and forward into the sweet spot while the stirrups catch your weight. See what arrangement of your thigh and platform most easily allows your weight to hang freely into the stirrups and drops your knee into the saddle's sweet spot, while your ankles stay relaxed and comfortable as they allow your weight into the stirrups.

Experiment with platform arrangements that most easily go along with various thigh and knee arrangements. Some will be easier on your back than others. Some will drop your shoulders toward the horse's neck, while some drop your tummy toward the horse's withers.

When you've found an arrangement that seems to use the fewest possible muscles, one that lets your bones line up along your horse's sides and above its spine most easily, ask yourself a couple of questions: Could I do this all day? What would give out first?

That will tell you what muscles are still involved in providing the skeleton some external support. That means there is some even easier way to line up your bones with gravity instead of using muscles to hold them in a certain place. If your back starts complaining, try raising your shoulders further away from the horse's neck, or pointing your tailbone more to the rear than downward. Or try letting the crown of your head extend further out of your spine. Try thinking about having very wide shoulders and rib cage.

If something in this exercise hurts or is just uncomfortable, you may have some joint(s) arranged to bear weight in a way contrary to how its ligaments are built, or some muscle might be working harder than its partners. Riding is going to involve more movement than we generally need in day-to-day living, so riding is where we want total freedom of motion. Discomfort is not the way to achieve that. Too often riders accept some small degrees of discomfort; some only get as far as finding a more tolerable level of pain. Pain is Nature's way of telling you to find another way to do something. Pain doesn't encourage free movement.

I promise you there is an arrangement that does not require any muscular effort. It is up to you to find what that is for your skeleton, on your horse, for today, at the halt.

When you think you've found a good arrangement, wait a bit. Can you gain another millimeter or ounce or thread of connection and ease by releasing a muscle somewhere? Just about when you think you've found effortlessness, another muscle will call for attention. That's exactly what we are waiting for. Say hello to your new muscle friend and invite it to relax with its buddies for a while. It may try to sneak back into its accustomed clench. Invite it, and everything else, to release again, and again. And again. There is a skeletal arrangement that does not require any muscles to clench at all, although some may do so just out of habit. They may have to clench rather a lot before you realize they have activated again. Keep looking for muscles to release. I want your physical arrangement at the halt to be truly comfortable and effortless. Think about clouds or flying birds or gentle breezes or anything airy and light.

After your heel release and your knee releast, you can sit in the saddle by opening your upper body/thigh angle. If you use your hip joint like the hinge that it is, rather than flexing your spine, you will end up feeling quite a bit taller. Open the angle between your torso and your thigh by releasing some muscles around your platform and all through your torso, but especially the front, from the area in front of the seatbones to collarbones. If you roll your spine out like a rug when you sit up instead of leaving your vertebrae stacked nicely and releasing your hip joints like opening a folding chair, I'm afraid you might have to start all over again. Think of it as another chance to try this "up on-your-toes, heel release, knee release" experiment and find more muscles to let go in order to sit fully in the saddle. Leave your weight dropping down the horse's sides and into your knees and ankles and further to your stirrups as you waft your torso upright. We will find out why later, but much of this release process is most easily taken care of by the deep interior muscles that are best operated by general mental directives like lightness, length, openness, freedom, and such. Another good directive would be to let the top of your head release away from your knees and to let your heels release away from your knees. Letting muscles release lets your skeleton move into its natural balance, without engaging more muscles to push our bones around into some external appearance.

WHAT DOES THIS TELL US?

This experiment is all about finding what feels most effortless and secure because you are working with your particular skeleton, ligaments, and muscles, and allowing gravity to help you, instead of fighting it. Finding your most comfortable and secure arrangement on a horse is a matter of letting your bones line up freely so they have the maximum potential for movement and therefore the most adaptable center of gravity and base of support. You can therefore stay well-balanced under the widest range of motion a horse offers. That means you are more secure.

A good seat is not a matter of holding a particular position. There is a big difference between adopting a pose versus providing yourself free range of motion so we work with gravity instead of against it. The highly desired depth of seat doesn't come from holding certain angles or from sitting heavily on the saddle. It comes from allowing our weight down along the horse's sides, so our upper body is well-supported and well-connected, so we can move fluidly with the horse. Depth of seat feels accurate and fitting, rather than stiff or heavy.

Pushing away from the horse is less stable than letting our weight just hang down either side of the horse. Shoving pressure on the stirrup is not the same as simply allowing our weight into the stirrup, where it will go anyway if we let it. Releasing our weight into the stirrups lets them hang nicely under our center of gravity. Pushed stirrups move as you may have found out if you lost your balance and tried to push on the stirrup to stay up, but instead crashed onto the horse's back all the faster. Pushing on a stirrup forces our knees upward and backward and probably shoves our platform backwards. A pushed-on leg is like a fence post, not like the shock absorber it can be. Our best security is to let our knees down and forward into the saddle's sweet spot and let your weight travel on toward the stirrups. The stirrups will catch your weight if you let them. That's what they are for. That requires softening our joints, not pressurring or locking them.

When you start finding muscles to release, many of the asymmetries you started with in your first seat inventory probably lessened or even went away, since they were likely caused by some contracted muscles. Some muscles may have become chronically tense, pulling your skeleton out of alignment. Looking for ways to release the top of our head up and away from each knee and each heel tends to work these things out, and we will see why that is in a later chapter. However, this new arrangement may feel lopsided to you, even if your observer sees or photos show a more symmetrical arrangement.

Interestingly, it is not at all uncommon for a horse to discover for itself that the easiest way to carry a rider whose muscles are no longer pulling the skeleton out of alignment and is therefore square to the ground in shoulders and hips and with equal weight in each stirrup is to stand very squarely itself. Consider what it may mean, then, whether your horse volunteers a square halt, or if it has to be "trained" to stand squarely.

We now have ways to explore how we are using our skeleton and muscles and how that influences our interface with the horse. We have also likely discovered that a more secure and comfortable seat is easier to find than we may have thought.

If a well-balanced seat is so easy to find, how did we arrive at going about things the hard way, only to get poorer results?

There are lots of reasons we may not have used our best skills in the course of learning to ride. Exploring both our physical patterns and our learning styles may shed light on our riding history to date. Learning more about them may open the doors to talents we may have overlooked or underutilized or thought didn't apply to riding. We may begin to see how our approach to riding can easily include our natural mastery. As we learn more about our ever-changing physical and mental patterns, we can discover easy ways to allow our natural mastery to shine.

These experiments will make it much easier for the horse to experience us the way we intend. You can use that ability to communicate with the horse in ways you may never have thought possible without years of practice.

CHAPTER 2

How People Move

Thought and emotion usually interact with the grace of well-trained dancers.
—Restack

*We are all addicts—the creatures of our habits . . . The knowledge of facts
and techniques is baseless without the grounding of self-knowledge.*
—Ruthy Alon

*How do we defeat the tendency toward what might be called a kind of wish fulfill-
ment in our senses, caused by a confusion between the event as intended and the event
as it really happened? How, in short, do we get rid of the bad habits that plague us?*
—Sarah Barker

Every sport has starting positions that offers the best alignment to perform
the moves needed in that sport. Football players need to do different things
than baseball players, so they use different starting positions. Ballet apparently
has five such starting positions, which makes me suspicious that ballet could
get complicated.

What has come to be called the rider's seat is simply the best skeletal
arrangement from which to most easily stay secure and to communicate
with the horse. A good seat is all about finding an arrangement for your
particular skeleton that allows all the ways you may need to move to adapt
to and enhance the horse's movement. A good seat gives the rider balance

and freedom of movement, and therefore security and responsiveness in our riding.

Our seat inventory probably showed a few asymmetries that have been stopping us from doing our jobs as riders in the most secure, easiest possible way. Our muscle releasing experiments may have shed some light on how you can easily allow your built-in mastery of balance and free movement to help your riding.

It is said of all masters of any art or sport that they make it look easy, even effortless. That's because masters really have found ways to do things more easily and effortlessly. If masters can figure out how to do something more easily and effortlessly, so can everyone else, or at least more easily and effortlessly than we non-masters presently go about things.

This isn't so much a matter of practicing more, but of practicing differently. Even the most rigorous practice schedule cannot make struggle look effortless. Practicing the same thing even more can end up confirming problems; practicing differently changes things.

How could we have developed relatively uncomfortable, less secure, and inefficient ways of riding? Any bodyworks practice like yoga, Feldenkreis, Pilates, etc., is likely to help riders clarify how our bodies do what they do. However, an approach called Alexander Technique (AT) studies physical movement and the mind/body relationship in ways that adapt directly to riding. I have yet to see an excellent performance in any sport that does not comply with the ideas and practices AT teaches.

Alexander Technique

Alexander Technique describes our physical patterns in ways that have come to have very different connotations now than when Mr. Alexander wrote about his discoveries. "Inhibition" in AT is a way to liberate your actions, which would have Freud spinning in his grave. "Non-doing" is a way to get things done, although some Eastern philosophers might take that as normal.

New ways of thinking about things we thought we understood keeps us young and curious.

AT offers many insights about why riders cannot seem to progress beyond a certain point, try as hard and as long as they might. It offers good explanations why many riders think they have gotten as far as they will ever get and either accept that limitation with all of its pitfalls, or quit riding. It also explains the sudden flashes of terrific riding that happen from time to time, and helps riders make better use of those golden moments. AT is a very effective way to discover your own personal change that makes a difference.

AT focuses on how our head, neck, and back work in relation to each other as the key to ease, symmetry, and balance. Just like problems in a house's foundation or walls will show up as problems in the roof, how the rest of our body operates is bound to show up in how our spine, neck, and head operate together.

Here are some useful AT ideas that go along with that primary observation.

Primary control—How a person's back, neck, and head interact says much, perhaps everything, about the entire body mechanism.

Our head can poise lightly atop the spine and lead the torso upward by releasing muscle tension that often pulls our head and neck down. Habitual misalignments elsewhere in the skeleton may also contribute to this tension.

How easily our head rests on top of our spine is a good indicator of how things are lined up elsewhere. It may offer clues about how our weight drops down the horse's sides and gets to our stirrups, too. Pulling everything toward our middle rather than releasing our head away from our heels, for example, will show up in our stirrup connection.

Looking at your seat inventory sheets, can you identify ways in which your spine could support your head more easily? Does that influence how your weight drops into your stirrups?

Use—The way we handle our own body, which is often far more roughly and constrained than need be.

How we use our bodies definitely influences the horse, since the horse operates on what it actually feels, not what we think it should feel, or what a book or video says it should feel. Horses cannot read books, but they sure can read people! Looking at your seat inventory sheets, can you identify any ways in which your use is less than efficient, effortless, and comfortable? It is a sure bet that as soon as you find a way to use yourself more effortlessly in your day-to-day activities, you are on your way to finding ways to become more effortless in your riding. Your seat inventory would change, too, as would how your horse experiences you as a rider.

Kinesthetic distortion—Feeling something is "right" because it is familiar.

We may become so accustomed to misalignments and tensions that they feel normal and symmetry and muscle relaxation feel abnormal and out of balance. Realigning this or that may feel quite "wrong," whereas instructions that seem to go along with what we are used to seem "right."

We may become very accustomed to some inefficiencies in riding, and our horses get used to them, too. This is especially true if we are generally satisfied with our riding, have lowered our goals to meet our current performance level, or decided we have reached the limit of our ability. These ideas tend to solidify our misperceptions about our riding, feeding a vicious cycle of ever-declining performance. Staying open to the possibility that there is always an easier, more effortless way to ride well is one way around our kinesthetic distortions.

End gaining—Getting so involved in the desired outcome that we don't know how we got the results we got, even if the way we went about things was the reason we didn't get where we were aiming to go.

It is easy enough to forget that the journey is as important as the destination. Especially under highly goal-oriented conditions, we can lose track of how fundamentally success depends on ease and freedom.

We often put up with discomfort if we think it will achieve some external goal, often to the point of learning to ignore pain. For example, adopting a certain form may or may not work with gravity according to your particular build. That is bound to set up uncomfortable stiffnesses that will convey to the horse and limit its performance, too.

> **Means whereby**—*How something turned out the way it did. How things got to where they are.*

You may or may not know why your ankles hurt, for example, until you realize how you are using them in conflict with their design. You may not know how to make a hurting ankle more comfortable until you take some time to explore different means whereby your ankles can operate as they are designed to operate.

> **Non-doing (also "un-doing")**—*Not trying to do what feels right, so as not to be limited to what we think we already know.*

Take time before taking unmindful action. Wait a bit before you decide you know the easiest possible way to do something. Give yourself a moment to check if your usual reaction is the best reaction. Keep a little space between habitual reaction and action, so new actions can arise.

> **Inhibition**—*Stopping habitual patterns so we can make new decisions and let effortlessness and lightness prevail.*

When you think you know how to fix your seat, don't always do that particular fix the way you have always done it before. There are probably ways to do it you haven't tried yet. Some may not work as well as your usual way, and others may turn out more successful that you ever thought possible. If all you ever do is what you did before, you can never do anything any better than you did it before.

Intention—The ultimate source of all action; what we mean to happen versus what we actually do.

Horses are masters at identifying our intentions and often react to them more accurately than they do to our more overt actions. That doesn't stop people from deciding a horse has a problem with crossing streams, for example, when it may be the rider who has concerns about whether the horse will willingly step into water or jump over it.

Intention is very active in our seat corrections, too. It is entirely possible that you meant to let your weight drop fully to the stirrups, but maybe what happened had a bit of a shove to it instead. Did you mean to drop your weight, or did you mean to get those heels down as far as you could make them go? Things can get confusing when our intentions are in conflict with each other and when instructions, internal or from a teacher, conflict with our conscious and our unconscious intentions.

Direction—Letting general mental instruction guide motion, rather than making specific muscles do specific things.

Mentally orienting the body, hopefully upward in the case of people and forward in the case of horses, but in both cases long and broad and open from heels to head as muscle tensions release.

General ideas like free movement, lightness, or awareness can be powerfully effective. Let your body parts do what they know how to do to contribute to a general idea, rather than pulling yourself here and there in bits and pieces.

Holding pattern—Habitual sets of muscle tension that tend to reappear, especially when we're not using general directives consistently.

If you often hold one shoulder up and twist your pelvis and put most of your weight on one leg when you are standing around, you will likely do that on horseback, too. If you pull your head down and scoop with your shoulders to stand up out of a chair, you will probably do something similar in other movements, too—like posting or cantering. These patterns often diminish when we use directives like poise, fluidity, grace, and lightness to guide our movements.

Setting up—Preparing for an action, especially by engaging unnecessary muscles, often according to our habitual holding patterns.

It is remarkably easy to set up a general tension when you feel the horse is about to do something, if you are about to be required to do something, or you feel something is amiss or out of your comfort range. When you set up, it is very likely that the muscles that have been getting a lot of practice in a certain holding pattern will kick in first and more strongly than other muscles. Setting up therefore often triggers holding patterns, perhaps along with general tension. Then you have to work all the harder to overcome tension to do what you wanted to do. In the meantime, what the horse felt was general tension, less mobility, and less adaptability.

Release—Letting balance and motion happen by relinquishing muscle contraction rather than by putting more muscles into action. Unlocking joints bound by unconscious muscle tension.

Release is the solution for holding patterns, resulting in easy primary control.

It is easier to lengthen your legs down horse's sides by releasing muscles around your hips, knees, or ankles so that your weight drops into the stirrups than it is to shove on the stirrups or to reach for them with your toes. It is easier to sit taller by releasing the muscles around your gut and rib cage than to hike your chest up again and again. It is easier to sit straight by releasing the muscles that may be pulling one side of your rib cage down, than it is to try to pull your rib cage into a certain spot. The horse will help you do all of these things and a thousand more, if you let it, as we will see.

For those who want drama and action in their body work, AT may seem too subtle a stage. If you are in the "no pain, no gain" camp, AT will change your mind about that.

AT offers a very comprehensive, sensible, and easy explanation and resolution for many physical limitations and habits. Excellent riders may not know they are in agreement with AT, but if you watch their primary control, you will see that they are very much in agreement with its principles. AT has not failed to agree with anything anyone would agree is ever-improving riding.

Reviewing your seat inventory lists and what you discovered through your up-on-your-toes/heel release/knee release experiments, you may well discover how these and other AT ideas can help you in your riding, as well as in your day-to-day use.

HUMAN MOTION 101

Ease and effortlessness come from working with the laws of Nature, especially gravity and balance. Gravity and balance keep us upright on foot, sitting, walking, running, dancing, etc. Gravity and balance will keep us on the horse, too, if we let them.

Our bones are designed to stack up one over the other to support each other and our center of gravity. When our bones are well lined up, support is nicely distributed over our skeleton. When we are still, muscle action is required only to keep lining our bones up when some movement, like breathing or a beating heart, shifts bones around. So, even standing still contains small balancing movements, mostly taken care of automatically.

Muscles provide some stability to joints; they can also allow bones to move or they can set bones in motion. Every moveable joint has one set of muscles that contract to close the joint angle (flexor muscles) and another set that contract to straighten the joint (extensor muscles). Every joint movement uses both sets of muscles. Motion is really a matter of balancing how flexors and extensors work in relation to one another.

When flexors contract to bend a joint, extensors must also release to allow the bend. The extensors can also limit and direct the movement so the joint doesn't flex too much or in the wrong direction.

When extensors contract to straighten a joint, flexors must release to allow and direct that. The flexors can also limit and direct the action so the joint doesn't overextend or move in the wrong direction.

Contracting both flexors and extensor at the same time immobilizes the joint in some position. If the flexors and extensors are equally engaged, the joint is still and aligned but is less free to move, depending on how active the muscles are. If the flexors and extensors are equally at rest, the joint is at rest and free to align with gravity but ready for motion.

A joint can be started in motion either by contracting flexors or by releasing extensors. For example, you can open your fist by extending your fingers or by relaxing any muscles that were pulling your fingers to your palm. Bonus question: What position do your fingers adopt if you relax all of your hand muscles? Does that change when your thumb is on top, or if your palm faces up or down?

We can use this idea many ways when we are experimenting with our seat. For example, you can rotate your knee inward toward the saddle by contracting the muscles that pull your bones that way, most of which are on the inside of your thigh. You can also allow your knee to rotate inward by releasing any muscles that point it to the front or outward. Most of those muscles are on the outside of your thigh and in the buttock area. Knee rotations in any direction may even involve some belly muscles. Certainly changing your pelvis orientation will change how your thighs most easily move in any direction.

Try clamping your buttock muscles, and you will find that tends to pulls your knee outward. You will also find it is tougher to rotate your knees inward if those muscles are clamped. Alternatively, relaxing your gluteal muscles will tend to drop your knees toward each other just as effectively as relying on thigh muscles to rotate or pull your knees toward each other when your buttocks are clamped.

Similarly, you can pull your chest up out of a slump, but it also works very well to release the muscles that were pulling your rib cage down in the first place. You can square your shoulders by releasing the muscles that were pulling one side down or holding one side up. You may well be unaware that some muscles were doing such things until you try this trick. But if you find that adopting some position or balance in your riding is difficult, look for the muscles that are pulling your skeleton out of alignment. Relaxing the muscles that are misdirecting things may be sufficient by itself and will certainly more easily allow whatever else you want to happen.

We tend to think motion must start by contracting muscles, but we can also allow and even start motion by releasing muscles. Obviously, moving by releasing muscles takes less physical effort than moving by contracting them. At the least, releasing tension in a joint before setting it in motion will make that motion easier and more fluid. We don't often think of releasing muscles as just as important a skill as contracting them, but we need both skills. Releasing muscles is easy and makes for smooth, fluid, graceful motion and makes way for more powerful or free-ranging movement, too.

HUMAN POSTURE 101

Free movement comes from how fluidly we use our muscles, but even the most fluid muscle use wouldn't turn out well if our skeleton isn't also well aligned.

If the skeleton is aligned with gravity, the bones support each other without much need for muscle action. Whether standing or in motion, any bone that is not lined up with a supporting bone below needs some kind of external support. Ligaments and maybe some muscles must be brought into play to keep a misaligned bone from getting too far out of line. One way to correct a misalignment is to use muscles to pull the bone back into line. Another way is to release muscles to allow a misaligned bone room to slip back into line. Once the bones are lined up again, hopefully both sets of muscles return to a resting state and the joint can just rest easily in its built-in support.

A person evenly relaxed through all muscles groups would have terrific posture, with the skeleton stacked up as it is built to do. Balance and good posture come at least as much from releasing muscle contractions so bones can line up the way they are designed as from contracting muscles to hold bones in place. Poor posture can be a sign of uneven muscle use, such as muscles pulling the rib cage down or hips or shoulders askew.

When skeletal misalignments are taken care of accurately and precisely, misalignments and muscle tension or slackness don't become a habit. But these skeletal realignments may not happen if we are not aware of a misalignment, or are unaware that a misalignment is a problem. We may even come to feel that some misalignment is normal, just because we have gotten used to it. We can easily get used to any physical arrangement that doesn't positively hurt—and some even that do!

We are generally familiar with the muscles we use to move, like arm and leg muscles. However, balance and overall skeletal alignment are mostly maintained by deep interior muscles. Such muscles are apparently difficult, perhaps impossible, to activate directly the same way we activate arm and hand muscles to pick something up, for example. These deep interior muscles are probably guided by general mental directives not unrelated to emotional states like pride or confidence, certainty or uncertainty, indifference or joy, and so on. Our typical posture may be more related to our prevalent moods than to specific tasks or exercises we do.

For example, good posture and free movement seem to arise by themselves when we are happy and confident, alert and open. We all know that part of trying to convince someone else we are happy, confident, etc., is to display good (not stiff) posture and fluid motion. When we are discouraged or nervous, bored or self-absorbed, we have to remind ourselves repeatedly to stand up straight, because our posture tends to return to some misaligned arrangement.

This could help explain why your best riding may often happen, seemingly automatically, when something wonderful just happened, or when you are sure you know how to handle a situation, or enjoy the challenge of the moment even if you're not entirely sure what to do, or when you are focused on something new, like a new course or a new horse (if you like that horse), to give just a few examples. It can also help explain why your riding does not seem to progress under other kinds of situations and often seems worse than ever, however much you practice. This is especially true if you believe it takes a lot of practice to progress, even though you may have experienced sudden forward leaps of progress that seemed to happen in an instant.

If we maintain a certain misalignment on or off the horse for some time, some muscles may weaken while others strengthen, like in any exercise we do a lot. So, some muscles may easily come to adopt a habitual slackness and get weaker while others maintain a habitual tension and get stronger, which AT calls a *holding pattern*. This uneven exercise of muscles can make a skeletal misalignment habitual even after our typical emotional state has changed. These habitual postures come to feel very familiar to us, even if they are not in fact the most effortless possible way of using our body. It is very easy to confuse familiarity with ease, which AT calls *kinesthetic distortion*. We may well not realize these postural habits have crept in, especially if we do not vary our day-to-day activities much. The postural habits you have on the ground will tend to show up in your riding, but postural habits are not written in stone. Posture that lets the skeleton line up well again can equalize the muscles again over time. Habitual muscular contractions can release and muscles that had become habitually slack can strengthen.

Certainly horses are aware of our balance and respond accordingly, so it is no great mystery that good posture and free movement are inherently rewarding in riding. I have also seen and felt the simple joy of riding, or even just being around my hoofed friends, banish these misalignments as if by magic. I have seen riders shed the apparent burden of work and home tasks as they arrive at the barn. It is very worthwhile to set discouraging matters aside before beginning a ride.

This indirect path of influencing our most basic balancing mechanisms and muscle use via our emotional state may be especially true for the deep spinal muscles, including the psoas we met during our seat inventory. The psoas can be tough to activate directly, even though they have everything in the world to do with our overall balance and how well our platform and contact area coordinate. That, in turn, is the majority of what a rider's seat is about.

Since riding is all about movement, the basis for a good seat in riding is to line up your bones so they are free to move however and whenever they may need to move. In your seat inventory and the heel release/knee release experiments, you may have come across some arrangements that look good but require muscles to maintain and thus don't allow your skeleton its full range of balanced motion.

Yet, the horse imparts motion to its rider with every step it takes. Riding is all about using to our advantage the movement of an animal built to shift half a ton with every stride, instead of trying to overcome it, as if that were even possible. Using muscles to clamp a skeleton into place despite the horse's movement is a big job! Since we are constantly being moved by the horse anyway, it is far easier to align ourselves so that the movement the horse is giving us improves our seat, rather than disturbing it.

There are a few reasons why we may not have learned to perfect that way of using a horse's movement quite yet, even though it is the most effective way to ride. Here are some of them.

Search Images

As the sayings go, perfect practice makes perfect, and practice makes permanent. Here are some ideas about why that is so.

How we mentally evaluate our own physical performance takes place largely outside of our logic centers, in the cerebellum rather than the neocortex. Deciding to do something is a different kind of thought than executing the decision and seeing if it is turning out as planned. This certainly has something to do with the mind/body connection. The motor patterns we learn, such as what it is like to ride a horse, have been called "search images." A search image is the idea we have of how an action is carried out and how it should turn out. Search images develop as we learn how to do things. They then apparently move into the cerebellum, beyond conscious control.

A search image could well include a general sense of how your body parts feel in relation to each other or how they relate to something else, like a tennis racket or a saddle. It may come to include how long something takes, what music would go along with it, how it would look to observers, or even how a performance might influence other areas of your life.

How well our observations and sensations matches our search image says a lot about whether we believe what we did was "right" or "wrong." Our search images may well be more compelling than judges' scores, rising vet bills, or physical pain.

The awkwardness, extra effort, and inaccuracies that go along with learning new things can become part of our standard for good performance as we build our search images. We can "learn" that a certain kind or amount of misalignment or extra effort or awkwardness is OK. *A less-than-perfect way of doing things can slip into subconscious control and become our standard for performance.*

Because we are not necessarily perfect at things at first, our skeletal arrangement and performance may only feel right (match our search image) when it is in fact out of alignment, or when we aren't using the most efficient, effortless way to go about things. This can easily fix a search image at a level of performance far below our actual ability. It may even make performance that is in fact better feel wrong just because it is not what we are used to.

When search images include inefficiencies and too much effort, some muscles may well get stuck with the job of constantly holding a joint in place or moving without ease, but still register as having done a good job. And there it is: our potential for a free range of movement is reduced and we didn't even know it.

Search images may well influence more than just skeletal alignment. Search images can include some pretty peculiar stuff. Try this:

Clasp your hands together by intertwining your fingers. You ended up with one thumb or the other on top. Now, interlace your fingers so that the other thumb is on top. Feels odd, doesn't it? There is nothing better or worse about one arrangement or the other. Nevertheless, one matches your search image for "clasped hands" better than the other.

A search image may well include things that are unrelated to the objective quality of performance, such as certain surroundings or trappings. So we may miss the fact that a horse is working in a way that would do very well in the dressage ring, just because it is under Western tack. A search image may well include something special about a time you did really well, like wearing gray socks under your boots. You might decide gray socks are a part of good performance. That's silly, of course. Everyone knows it's mismatched socks that really work.

Whatever matches our search image is what we tend to feel is the right way to do things or the right way to look. We tend to do them automatically and evaluate ourselves and others accordingly, even if our search image is not entirely sensible.

For example, riders may figure some bumping in the saddle is just the way things are in the sitting trot. That has been their experience of the sitting trot, nothing very terrible has happened yet, everyone else complains about the horses' rough gaits, too, and the instructor doesn't seem seriously to expect anything else. Bumping in the saddle can become part of a rider's idea of what a sitting trot is like. Bumping in the saddle can remain part of the riders' personal search image for the sitting trot even if they have been told or observed that bumping in the saddle doesn't need to be part of sitting a trot, but do not have the personal experience of sitting a trot smoothly.

In that case, a sitting trot that *didn't* include bumping may well not be recognized as a sitting trot! A rider could honestly assume that the few trot strides that didn't include bumping must not have been trot strides, simply because they didn't include bumping. I have seen more than one rider assume the horse was not trotting, instead of realizing they just sat a trot very comfortably. As illogical as it seems, this sort of thing is very common. A search image that includes what is actually a flaw can even shut out experiencing our own better performances.

Every personal experience of even marginally better performance can adjust our search images upward. It doesn't really require more than one stride of excellent performance to revise our search image far upward, and we all hit upon those occasionally. They are worth gold!

Staying open to the possibility that there could be a smoother, more poised, faster, easier, happier, prouder, more elegant, or in any way better way of riding means we will never be limited by our previous performance because of unquestioned—and therefore subject to improvement—search images.

Effective Personal Riding Standards

The learning skills riders need to find an easy and smooth connection with the horse are often left to students to discover for themselves. Learning how to tell if the way we ride benefits our horses is not often addressed early in our riding career, either. Especially as beginners, riders are more often taught and praised for external form or a specific task. Describing and practicing good form and performing specific tasks isn't wrong, but it may be less helpful than learning how to ride according to your horse's experience of you as a rider and using comfort and ease in form and tasks as signs of success.

Using the interplay between horse and rider as a sign of success is a very different learning experience than checking an inventory list of what hands, heels, and hips "should" be doing. It is also different than evaluating performance according to achieving a specific task such as reaching a particular spot in the arena, regardless of how tensely or unwillingly that got done. This confuses the means and the ends of good form and accurate performance. Easy and smooth riding also looks good to observers and feels good to the rider and the horse, even if details of good form may vary from person to person. Easy and smooth riding will improve accuracy along the way, too.

Not surprisingly, many students who try to force a certain form, even if it is "right," end up learning without specifically being taught that some restriction, tension, discomfort, or even pain seems inevitable in riding well. They may learn that trots involve bumping on the saddle and directing a horse basically means pulling reins and kicking the horse's sides, however gently. The hope is that it will all eventually get easier after they learn how to ride better, or ride a better horse.

This is odd, since the hallmarks of mastery are effortlessness, grace, ease, and freedom of motion, even when (especially when!) the task at hand gets as fast and furious as a timed jump-off or barrel race.

General directives like ease, effortlessness, and attention to how our horse experiences you as a rider can effectively guide how your body arranges the details of things. This is comparable to the way a spring day puts more of a bounce in your step than a blizzard does (unless you really enjoy blizzards). Consider how differently you would go about walking down the street if your goal was to leave as light a footprint on the pavement as possible versus leaving heavy footprints or footprints of a certain pattern. Things would be different again if your goal is to get to the end of the block as quickly as possible regardless of how the pavement is impacted.

So, we all know how to adjust the details of our way of doing things by using a general directive. Exploring the details of how the body achieves an overall approach to a task can be interesting and useful, but it is not entirely necessary to get the job done. We can use a few lucky moments of being free-moving, light, balanced, and graceful with our horse to explore the details of how that happened, but it's the overall directive that produced those details in the first place. General directives are very effective means whereby we allow the details to fall into place.

We can analyze the details that add up to a good ride (or a bad one), but the sum is always something greater than the parts. The only tool riders need to upgrade a search image is their own nervous system, which they bring along on every trail ride, jump course, reining pattern, or cattle job, when an instructor might not be available or allowed by the rules of the game to help.

Everything changes when our interface with the horse is our primary source of feedback while learning to ride. Putting priority on specific tasks or appearances often comes at the expense of sensitivity to that interface. Indeed, I have often encountered riders with years of experience who have less sense of the horse's gaits than absolute beginners and less than I suspect they may have had when they were beginners themselves. Yet, the success of specific tasks and appearance is a direct result of our interface with the horse. Very likely, our idea of what connecting with horses would be like was a large reason most riders took up the sport. Certainly, our horses will know when the rider's priority changes from specific performance or appearance to a comfortable, secure, and communicative interface with the horse under ever wider ranges of performance. Luckily, our bodies already know all about this, too, so this shouldn't be difficult to apply (or regain) in our riding.

Everything else will follow from the quality of our interface with the horse, how the horse must experience us as riders, including lovely form that works effectively for your particular build and creates virtually automatic adjustments to the horse's movements.

It may be that *what* you have been doing (jumping a certain height or doing a certain figure) has been more emphasized in your riding far more than how you are doing it (gracefully, effortlessly). You will get what you train for. The general qualities that mark all masters, like effortlessness and grace and poise and accuracy in the way we go about things, will lead us to mastery. Developing (or regaining) that aspect of the quality of your work combined with technical knowledge of your favorite sport is likely to make for a quantum leap forward in your and your horse's performance. Why not start out or start again the way you intend to go?

FORM, EXPERIENCE, AND SCOPE OF ATTENTION

Picturing how your riding looks to an observer can be a valuable exercise. Imagining how it would look if you were riding as well as a rider you admire, or on a day you were really on your game, can be a very effective way to upgrade your search image and give you more practice in using general directives to guide your performance. Instruction that emphasizes how a seat looks may ultimately allow riders to develop the smooth and easy connection with the horse good form is supposed to give us. Form and how the horse experiences us as riders work hand-in-hand, but they are not necessarily equal as guides for action.

One approach approves of a certain appearance; the other approves of a certain quality of connecting with the horse. One approach plays to an outside audience; the other plays to an audience of one—the horse you are on at the moment. One emphasizes the technical standards we meet in our riding; the other emphasizes the reasons we ride.

Horses cannot know and do not care how their rider looks to observers. Horses don't care if your heels are down, but they do care if you are easy to carry and understand. Horses don't care if your hands are down, but they do care how the bit feels in their mouth.

However it looks, a perfectly consistent interface would feel very still and comfortable to the horse. Carrying a good rider would be like wearing perfectly fitted shoes. Changes in our interface that we don't feel but the horse does feel lead to misunderstandings. Learning to maintain a riding posture (often mentally translated as "hold a pose") before we learn to use the elastic interplay between the horse and the rider as our sign of success tends to hide that interplay below our sensory radar. Learning a posture first can make this interplay seem secondary or more advanced. It can make the horse a kind of moving platform on which to perform certain physical gymnastics until we learn to ride.

As it happens, our bodies will tend to arrange themselves into excellent form in riding if we are guided by the concept of how the horse experiences us as riders. Just tuning in very closely to your interface with the horse puts you in a receptive, exploratory mode, rather than a broadcast mode. That alone changes the neurological pathways we use. It changes your signs of success from *what* you are doing to the quality of *how* you and your horse are going about your jobs. I'd rather have more quality than just more work.

Close attention to details, like noticing how a particular joint is operating at the canter, can reveal how that influences our overall balance and fluidity or how it compares with the same joint on the other side, for instance. How narrow or wide a scope of attention we use makes a big difference in what we learn, but nagging at ourselves often involves a narrow scope of attention on details that we think are wrong or soon will be. Close attention to a bigger picture, like how the horse experiences being ridden at the canter, brings up different matters, including learning how well our bodies can take care of the details that add up to a larger picture.

We can also use our ability to change our scope of attention to help our horses by looking at how details of their performance contribute to their overall performance. Let's say we discover the horse is using one hind leg differently than the other one. That could explain its varying response to our aids, its lack of muscle in some areas, why one side of the saddle has more rub spots on it than the other, why the sweat stain on your left boot is different than the one on your right boot, and how that way of going is reflected in the larger picture.

We use narrower and wider scopes of attention all the time, but not necessarily consciously or effectively. We can slip into a particular scope of attention without realizing it and sometimes get stuck there. Everyone is better at either the broader or narrower focus. We need both, so practice them both, and practice switching between them.

The horse's experience of us as riders determines how well our riding will turn out, so that is a sensible way to evaluate our performance. I am assuming we wish the horse to experience us as balanced, welcoming, trustworthy, fun, prepared, clear, knowledgeable, creative, and so on, according to the horse's needs, just the way we would want our own gym teachers and religion teachers to be. How the horse experiences us as riders becomes the measurement of our success. Body control becomes a means to an end, not an end in itself.

The Tricky Parts about Learning to Ride

Our feedback loop as riders is unlike that of any other sport. Unlike baseballs or tennis balls or bowling balls, horses can do other than what we direct them to do. We may give aids "perfectly" and get different results than we expected. If we give aids "incorrectly," the horse may figure out what we mean anyway. This is like playing basketball with a ball that can learn that getting through the hoop is a big deal to its handler and its team. I wonder how much a ball like that would be worth?

Horses' responses to us include their mental qualities and personal histories, so their feedback to us is not always as clear as where a ball ends up when you throw it. Even the most thoroughly trained horse will adapt to each rider's talents and foibles. As riders, we must have insight into our own physical and mental workings as well as the horse's, lest we be misled about how well balanced our seat is or how accurate our aids are. Blaming poor performance on a bat or ball is a delusion much less available to baseball batters or tennis players, but it can be tricky to sort out if a horse missed a jump because it screwed up on its own, or because we interfered with it or guided it poorly. This takes considerable personal insight and character from riders, since it is possible and sometimes even correct to attribute less than perfect results to the horse's limitations or excellent results to our abilities.

Another unique thing about riding is that much of a rider's movement is not initiated by the rider, but by the horse. Gym mats, baseballs, and tennis rackets don't do that. Riders must factor in both how the horse's motion impacts us and how we impact the horse's motion.

Now, here's an interesting trick. Change the word "impact" in that sentence to "influence" and notice the very different sense conveyed about what riding is like and what feedback would be of interest:

Riding is all about motion, both how the horse's motion influences us and how we influence the horse's motion.

Change "influence" to "assist," and we get another picture of things:

Riding is all about motion, both how the horse's motion assists us and how we assist the horse's motion.

Simply changing how we think about things can confirm our existing ideas or open new territory. Plus, muscles do react when we just think about doing something or imagine something happening. It's quite possible for us to get upset or happy about things that never happened outside our own imagination. This physical reaction to the mind's eye is quite universal. It may be so slight that we don't usually feel it, but I have no doubt that horses know all about these things. Our thoughts, moods, imaginings, hopes, and fears do influence us physically, and therefore influence the horse. Improving your riding starts with acknowledging that there is always some way in which your riding could be better, and that riding better is easier.

We have taken a close look at our basic physical arrangement on horseback and at how that may relate to our learning habits and our mental and even emotional habits. Riding is as much a mental game as a physical one. Sensing or imagining the difference between what is happening and how it could be more effortless, efficient, poised, and fluid is a matter of curiosity. Curiosity is all we need to be on the road to continual improvement at whatever sport we like.

Now, let's see how these ideas about human motion and learning skills work when the horse is in motion.

CHAPTER 3

Opportunities in Equine Motion

You cannot step twice into the same waters,
for other waters are always flowing over you.
—Heraclitus

Sweet are the uses of adversity . . .
—Shakespeare, *As You Like It*

Riders want security, comfort, and effectiveness in all horse sports. We have found we can use gravity rather than just muscular effort to discover a comfortable and secure seat at the halt. We also know more now about how we can use to our advantage detailed and broad exploration of our own sensory experience of our interface with the horse. We know more about how physical habits may have been interfering with our best riding, but that habits are not written in stone, since we are constantly learning and experiencing new aspects of riding. With these important mental and physical exploratory skills in hand, let's use them to explore our seat in motion.

Horses are big animals! We tend to get used to that quickly, but staying on at the same time we are supposed to control the movement of such a big animal may well have seemed the central problem on our first rides. It may have seemed necessary to work against the horse's movement to stay on the horse or to give aids. It may have seemed safer to keep the horse's movement within the range we can physically overpower to stay on. It may come to seem that getting tossed around by the horse's movement is just part of riding. Our reflexes are wired to counteract such sources of insecurity by pulling our muscles together and restricting our range of motion, which in turn restricts the horse's motion. A horse that responds unexpectedly quickly to our aids can trigger our resistance to the very movement we asked for.

These are common vicious cycles until we get the hang of using the horse's movement to our advantage for both security and communication. Without that skill, we can't much wonder why horses are constrained in their movement under saddle, dull to our aids, and perform at less than their best.

It seems obvious to me that the least a rider can do for the horse is not to be part of the horse's problem. The rider can be a reliable source of guidance instead of the horse's main problem. After the horse can move as well with a rider as without one, we can start thinking about refinements specific to the sport we like.

The horse's motion can be our biggest resource instead of the main problem for riders. When we use the horse's motion to help us get more secure with each stride, every move a horse makes is a source of security instead of a disturbance to overcome. When we also use the horse's motion to create our aids, our aids secure our seat instead of disturbing it. Our aids can then assist the horse's many natural ways of balancing itself, as the term "aids" rightly suggests, instead of disturbing our horses' already superb athleticism. We can use the horse's motion positively to secure our seat and to make our communications to the horse accurate and timely.

Let's look closely at how we can use the horse's motion to our advantage for security and communication. That starts with looking at a horse in motion.

The basic unit of movement for the horse is always the same, regardless of the gait or sport. Starting from the moment when the hind leg is grounded directly under the pelvis, the hind leg rotates backwards and then pushes off the ground. The pelvis transmits that push forward through the barrel and along the horse's spine to the horse's neck and head. This movement swings the horse's center of gravity as if it were a bag of water suspended under the horse's spine, usually a bit behind the shoulders. A foreleg catches whatever weight is transferred in its direction as the bag of water/center of gravity sloshes around. Then the other hind leg repeats the process in a sequence specific to each gait.

The horse's head and neck act like a balancing pole and also move around to collect sensory information.

The horse's center of gravity shifts with these movements. Even breathing sloshes that bag of water/center of gravity around somewhat. I doubt it is ever 100 percent still.

If a rider's center of gravity is lined up with the horse's center of gravity, the rider's weight will be distributed over the horse's four feet in the same proportion as the horse's own weight is distributed over them. That lets the horse do its job the way the horse was built to do it. If a rider's center of gravity is not lined up with the horse's center of gravity, more weight is transferred through the horse's body to a hoof in a way unlike when the horse isn't being ridden. A horse carrying an out-of-balance rider must alter its natural stance and footfall, which makes its job more difficult. The horse has to operate differently than it would on its own and differently than it would carrying a rider who stays more in line with the horse's center of gravity.

Riders who are always out of balance one certain way, perhaps because of some holding pattern that causes a persistent asymmetry, will consistently put an extra burden on some rather localized part of the horse. The horse will no doubt adapt to a rider's consistent misalignment, but that risks setting up a chronic misalignment in the horse, too. This cycle creates undesirable consequences to the horse's performance and health just as it does to ours.

Riders who change their balance without consistency may not set up chronic, localized misalignments in horses, but it must be like trying to carry a sack of Mexican jumping beans. Horses with such riders could logically decide that most changes in how they experience riders are not meant as communication from the rider, and that it is best to keep their motion to a minimum. This is more likely for horses that carry a variety of riders, each unbalanced in a different way.

A good seat would keep the rider secure and keep the rider's balance consistent with the horse's center of gravity unless the rider intended otherwise. A good seat uses the horse's movements to create security. The rider is easier for the horse to carry, so it can use its talents at least as fully as it does at liberty.

A rider moving perfectly with the horse looks very still, but that is an optical illusion. If we put a life-sized statue of a rider on a horse, we would see that being rigid is not the same as being still in relation to the horse's movement. The statue won't stay on the horse very long once the horse starts moving, either. We could try bolting the statue to the saddle, but the statue would rub and bump against the horse with every step it took. Bolting a statue to the saddle is not unlike what happens when riders try to lock into a position. Trying to maintain a rigid, static position while the horse is in motion is tiring for a rider, and it restricts rather than promotes the horse's athleticism. The horse would no doubt prefer to carry a statue made of rubber, but something would still be missing.

No rigid, inanimate thing can take action to secure itself on a moving horse . . . but people can.

We can take advantage of the horse's motion to secure our seat with every step. We can use the horse's motion to our advantage, or we can let each step push us out of a dynamic alignment and cause us to engage extra muscles to stay attached to the horse.

Riding a horse in motion can instead be like playing on a swingset when we were kids. Our parents or friends kept the swing going for us, much like the horse gives us a lot of swing when we ride. On the swingset, you didn't have to do anything but let your buttocks connect with the swing seat and enjoy the ride. We easily developed a feel for what kind of swing each push was going to create. As our balancing skills developed, we began to enjoy being given larger and larger swings. Before long, it was "Look, Ma! No hands!"

We learned quite readily how to direct the swing by exaggerating the same movements we were already using to balance with the swing. We learned how to put a little twist left or right into the swing by amplifying the movement on one side more than the other. We also learned how to work against the existing swing to shut down the motion. We most likely learned to do all these things without anyone teaching it specifically.

So, luckily, the human body is already a master at going with the swing and directing it. Using the swing of the horse's movement is much more fun than getting tossed around every time a horse takes a bigger step than we can overpower. Every stride a horse takes gives us opportunities to become more secure and more comfortable, even the strides we don't expect or understand.

THE HORSE'S MOTION
AS A RESOURCE

We can use every move a horse makes to improve our security and make it easy for the horse to do the job we want it to do, too. These two goals are 100 percent compatible with each other.

We know now that just letting our weight hang down the horse's sides into the stirrups can contribute a lot of security for a lot less effort than gripping on the horse or shoving on the stirrups. We know that letting our muscles release our joints allows the best skeletal alignment for our center of gravity to remain within our base of support. We know that when our torso rises up symmetrically out of our hip joints and both legs drop freely out of both hip joints, our weight hangs evenly down both sides of the horse. Our knees can drop down and forward into the saddle's sweet spot and release our weight to the stirrups through our flexible ankles. We know now that how our weight transfers to our stirrups can be viewed as a summary of our balance on the horse from heels to head, just like how our weight gets to our feet and how easily our head rests on the top of our spine says much about our balance and alignment on the ground.

We found earlier that securing ourselves at the halt means finding the arrangement that lets gravity do its job best. The question, then, is how to use the horse's motion to help our weight drop down and forward along the horse's sides and into the stirrups and to let us stay light and aligned above the horse when it is moving.

We can tell if we are using the horse's motion to our advantage in two ways:
* Our platform (if we are seated in the saddle) and our contact area (always) will be 100 percent consistent in their connection to the horse; and,
* Our weight will be consistent in the stirrups.

We have seen how easily bips, pops, friction, rubs, and flops can become part of our unconscious standard for acceptable riding, especially if we are guided by appearance rather than how the horse experiences us as riders. But if we use the horse's motion well, there wouldn't be any rubs, bumps, rolling around, or friction. Sounds comfortable and secure to me!

You May Move Now

Get yourself arranged well at the halt, perhaps using the heel release and knee/hip release experiments we did in the first chapter. Check out your interface with the horse, how your weight is distributed over your platform, how your contact area is arranged, and how your weight lies on the stirrups so you rest lightly and consistently in the saddle.

As before at the halt, please don't try to fix something you think is wrong during this experiment. We want to take time to get familiar with "mistakes" so we don't stay body blind to them. What we think is a mistake might offer some good information even if it isn't what we are looking for at the moment, and might be exactly what is needed in some circumstances.

Try this experiment at the walk:

Without using your regular aids (instead, cluck, ask someone to lead your horse—be creative but don't use any of your regular aids), get the horse to walk for ten or twenty strides. It doesn't matter where the horse goes, other than not going over a cliff or walking into other horses or some other unsafe thing. It doesn't matter what kind of walk the horse offers, although that is something of interest to observe as we experiment.

All you have to do while your horse walks around is to check your platform and contact area, your total interface area with the horse. Are there any bips, pops, rubs, rolls, or flops anywhere along your interface with the horse? What's different from one moment to the next? If there are any changes, even tiny millimeters and ounces, how do those changes correspond to the horse's movements?

Next, check the details of your overall interface. Start with your platform. You can use the first Platform Inventory Sheet, page 63, to make some observations.

After a dozen or so strides, stop the horse, noting any changes in your interface with the horse while the horse is halting, too. Common examples are rolling around on your seatbones, rising out of the saddle to pull harder on reins, lower legs swinging forward or backward, or tightening your thighs or knees. Do a few more walk/halts again, getting more and more sensitive to any changes in your interface with the horse, including when these changes first occur and any patterns you see cropping up. You might also notice times when your body reflexively responds to something the horse does or what your reflexes do if you fall out of balance or rhythm.

Halt for a minute and run through the "up on your toes, heel release, knee/hip release, slide into the saddle" experiment from the first chapter, and get yourself nicely arranged again. Do that one more time, but leave things at the "up on your toes, heel release, knee/hip release" stage, without sitting fully in the saddle. That will put you in something like a half-seat, or two-point seat or jumping position, as this is variously called.

With your seatbones slightly out of the saddle, your knees cozied into the sweet spots on the saddle, and your weight well released to the stirrups, take a look at your contact area. The area in front of your seatbones may be in touch with the saddle depending on your stirrup length, but this experiment will emphasize the contact area more than the platform. Just like at the halt, please hold a bit of mane so you can soften the thunk if you lose your balance and drop into the saddle. Walk around again a bit and check out any changes in your contact area as the horse moves. Use the second Contact Area Inventory Sheet, next page, to note down your observations.

In this half-seat, ask yourself: could I do this all day? What would get tired first? That tells you what is working harder than it needs to. What happens if you just stop using those overworked muscle(s)? There is an arrangement that eases any overworked muscles. You might well have to run through a few experiments to find it, but each experiment can tell you something new. That's all we are after.

A single photo can't identify any patterns of change in your interface with the horse as it moves. Video would work better than a series of still photos, but what you feel is more important than what someone else might see.

Platform Inventory Sheet

Check this out	Notes
Are the three points of your platform connected to the horse's back or the saddle the same as they were at the halt?	
Did your platform interface with the horse change at all when the horse started moving?	
As the horse is walking along, can you feel more pressure under one seatbone and then the other, for example?	
Are your seatbone(s) or the area in front of your seatbones shifting on the saddle, or rolling back and forth over the same place in the saddle? If you aren't sure, try slipping your fingertips between your seatbone(s) and the saddle.	

Contact Area Inventory Sheet

Check this out	Notes
Is your contact area the same as at the halt?	
Did your interface with the horse's sides change at all when the horse started moving?	

Contact Area Inventory Sheet *(cont.)*	
Can you feel your thigh(s), knee(s), or calves getting closer to or further from the saddle or horse? Are they shifting up or down? You can use the fingertip test now, too.	
Is your connection with the stirrups the same all the time, or is it intermittent, or more on one stirrup and then the other?	
Are there any times when it feels like the saddle is dropping away from any of your body parts (less connection or touch or pressure) or pushing on a body part (more connection or touch or pressure)?	
Is there a pattern to how your interface with the horse changes? Is there a pattern to these changes?	

Return to a full seat and check out your platform and contact area again, or go back and forth between a full seat and a half-seat. The more you do this experiment, the more sensitive you will become to how consistent your platform and contact area are and how the horse's movement influences that.

We can't possibly know what is the most right or the most wrong yet, but if something is hurting even a little, please go ahead and find a more comfortable arrangement. Don't fall into the trap of accepting a level of discomfort you think you can live with.

It is very easy to bypass details of our interface with the horse in motion after we found a great starting arrangement and instead try to adopt a pose. Any bips, pops, and rubs that crop up when the horse starts moving are signs that the horse is moving more than the rider. A great starting arrangement is not an end in itself. It is just a good place from which to allow motion. Paradoxically, you may feel more still when you allow the thousand tiny movements that define a smooth interface with the horse with no bips or pops or rubs. That means you are more fluid, and moving with the horse instead of being a statue.

These walking experiments give you as much time as you like to discover how much, when, where, and what kinds of connections and disconnections you have with your horse in motion. The horse will develop as much sensitivity or insensitivity to these connections and disconnections as the rider develops.

What Do We Know Now That We Didn't Know Before?

You have probably discovered that following the horse's motion, as this is called, involves a thousand small movements with every stride. Focusing on your platform and contact area for a few strides may have made changes in your connection to the horse more obvious to you. Or, you may have realized it is much more consistent and symmetrical than you expected. You may have made some discoveries about the interplay between the smaller details of your interface and the larger picture.

The general feeling of how everything works together as a unit for lightness and effortlessness is a reliable guide. Using a whole body sense often leads to individual body parts making automatic adjustments on their own. Your body is a master at these small adjustments that promote an overall physical arrangement.

You have a lot more sensory information than you had before. You have more practice at sensing how the horse's motion affects you. You have gained a sense of what the horse is experiencing as you ride. That's worth gold. Once you start looking for it, it becomes obvious that a horse is often responding to things we didn't know were happening, but of which the horse was very well aware.

We can also use the horse's motion to tell us what the horse is doing, simply by paying close attention to how the horse moves us. So, walk around again and we will check out how to tell what the horse is doing by how the horse's motion moves our platform and, after that, our contact area.

GOING UP?

As you walk around, what aspect of the horse's movement lifts your platform? Try saying "now" every time you feel motion lift your platform.

Make sure that you attend to each step. It is very easy to catch a sense of this lifting motion for a few strides and then go off in a rhythmic singsong of our own that ends up out of time with what the horse is really doing. Just because the horse took three consistent steps in a row says very little about the fourth step. The chances are high that the horse's strides aren't exactly consistent. Staying in time with the horse when its strides change proves that you are reporting what is happening instead of what you think should happen. Remain in a receptive, reporting mode. You might feel momentary increases in pressure under one or both seatbones. It might feel like the seat of the saddle is kind of tapping your seatbones. It might feel like the horse is trying to push your seatbone(s), which is exactly what is happening.

You can tell when the horse's back is lifting if you and the horse bump into each other, but that's a sign that your platform is rather rigid over the horse's back as it swings. If your platform is more mobile and smoothly connected with the horse's motion, you can tell what the horse is doing by how its motion changes your motion, instead of when you and the horse bump into each other.

If your platform is in steady contact with the saddle because your spine is flexing with the horse's movement, you will feel your waist and back flexing with each step. You might sense your waist flexing, or your rib cage lifting and dropping. Your platform might also roll somewhat in the saddle. Your points of contact with the saddle might shift around over various parts of your platform, even if your platform stays in the same place in the saddle. Or your seatbones might slide along the skin between your seatbones and the saddle. That all still counts as rolling.

If your platform is still in the saddle because your spine is quiet, one vertebrae supporting the next, and your joints are mobile, your weight can fall consistently over your platform. The angles between your torso and your thighs (hip joints), your thighs and your shins (knees), and your shin and the top of your foot (ankles), will flex and rebound like shock absorbers in rhythm with the horse's steps. You have a much greater range of motion if you leave your spine stacked up and let your hip joints play than if you flex your spine to move your hips. The mobility of all leg joints helps keep our platform consistent on a moving horse more easily than using our spine in ways it is not designed to do.

Letting your leg joints rather than your spine absorb the horse's motion would be like standing on the ground with your knees somewhat bent and allowing someone to push one or both seatbones higher and more forward. That would somewhat open the angles between your upper body and your thigh(s), and open the angles of your knees and ankles. You would stand a bit taller, whereas flexing your spine pulls things toward your middle. Notice also that your weight can stay quite consistent over your feet if you let your joints roll around like ball bearings. It's when your joints aren't free that your weight shifts from the back to the front of your foot as your platform moves.

It's pretty obvious which way of moving is going to be most comfortable for the horse. If you have a question about that, try getting down on all fours and have someone take a 20-pound weight and press it or tap it or thunk it or roll it or rub it around on your back for about an hour. Even if that irritation is muffled, like a well-fitting saddle might do, it would be much nicer if it didn't happen at all.

Notice also that the horse's back lifts twice every walk stride. You might need a mirror, an observer, or a video at first, but see if you can answer this bonus question: What are each of the horse's hind legs doing when the horse's back is lifting your platform?

LET'S THINK ABOUT THIS FOR A MOMENT

Now we know that the horse's hind leg motion at particular phases of the walk steps raises the horse's back. We can feel that lift by how the horse's motion influences us.

If we don't allow the lifting movement to change our position at all, we can feel the saddle tapping on our platform. If we absorb the horse's motion mainly by flexing at the waist, our platform rolls in the saddle and there is relatively little flexion in our hip and leg joints. If our platform rests steadily in the saddle by absorbing the motion mainly with our mobile joints, the angles between our upper body, thighs, lower legs, and feet all change as our platform, torso, and head are moved up and away from our feet, although our vertebrae stay aligned, as they were designed to be.

How the horse's motion effects our interface with the horse can tell us everything we need to know. Ask yourself these questions:

What lets your platform stay 100 percent consistent with the horse in these lifting moments? What allows the horse to move you most easily? What would prevent you allowing these movements? How can you tell that? How quickly does your horse sense and respond to changes in your platform? Are its responses consistent? These are all points of interest we can use to get to know our horses better and see things more accurately from their point of view.

We also know now that the horse's back is highest at the walk when its hind legs are directly under its pelvis. This happens twice every walk stride. That happens once about midway through the left hind leg's support phase, which is also when the right hind is in its flight phase. The horse's back and hindquarters sink somewhat when the left hind is farthest behind the horse as it pushes off and the right hind leg is swinging farthest forward to touch down. The back and hindquarters lift again when the

Comparing two phases of the walk. The horse's hindquarters are higher when the hind feet are just below the pelvis than when the hind feet are touching down or pushing off.

right hind is midway through its support phase and the left hind is in its forward flight phase.

Once we are used to feeling how the lift and the drop of the horse's back corresponds to what the horse is doing with its feet at the walk, we can figure out every other part of the walk, too. We will take a close look at each of the gaits later, but for now we can use the walk to train our sensory systems to tell us what we can't see about the horse's movement when we are in the saddle.

USING THE LIFT FOR SECURITY AND COMMUNICATION

Using the horse's motion to help secure our seat drops our weight into the stirrup from high in the leg, allows our knees to drop down and forward, and lets our ankles relax and flex like shock absorbers. If we let our weight drop into the stirrup through mobile hips, knees, and ankles, our heels will sink very prettily and anchor our contact area as well, which is really the point of it all.

Using the lifting motion of the horse's back can help us get more secure and comfortable a few ways.

We can use the lift of the horse's movement to allow the saddle to reconnect with our platform, should that connection get lost. Since the horse's back lifts twice every walk stride, we have two opportunities every stride to allow the horse's back to reconnect smoothly with our platform. This is easier than sitting heavily and tightly on the top of the saddle.

We can use the lift of the horse's movement to open our hip and leg angles if they got cramped, almost like a mini-massage. Mobile hips, knees, and ankles let our weight stay consistent in the stirrups while the horse's motion lifts our platform away from our feet, which can help us sit more elegantly. Letting our legs lengthen by releasing muscles from the top of our thighs so our leg joints play freely allows a consistent connection with the stirrup helped by gravity; doing so doesn't strain our joints and doesn't push us farther away from the horse.

Allowing the stirrups to catch our weight by letting our legs slip down along the horse's side as its back lifts is quite different than pushing on the stirrups. Braced ankles and knees hold our platform away from the saddle, and the horse may well encounter an immobile platform when it lifts its back. If our legs joints are rigid, the upward lift of the platform will also carry our legs up and away from the stirrup. That can leave riders shoving their heels down or searching for their stirrups with their toes but without letting their knees slip lower. This pits one set of muscles against another, using more effort to get less result.

Pushing on the stirrup usually goes along with pushing our buttocks backwards, which is contrary to the horse's back motion. Pushing on the stirrup usually makes knee(s) rub on the saddle instead of maintaining a light, consistent connection as the saddle moves. Pushing on the stirrups often moves our knees up and/or back, away from the saddle's sweet spot, and we end up reaching for the stirrups with our toes again. There might be pressure on the stirrup, but not weight.

Letting your thighbone turn toward the horse instead of trying to connect with the horse by gripping also requires releasing muscles all around the hip joints. Pulling the tops of your thighs together to grip the seat of the saddle narrows the space between your two hip joints. That essentially squeezes you farther away from the saddle. Instead, relax so the horse's lifting motion reconnects the saddle with your platform.

Trying to grip the top of the saddle often goes along with tushie-tucking, gripping especially with the back of your thigh(s), knee(s) or calves, or turning out both knees (or either knee). If we are tight or squeezed together at the tops of our thighs, the horse's lift tosses us out of the saddle or rolls our platform a bit if the horse offers anything like free forward movement. Unfortunately, that tends to convince us all the more that we have to grip instead of allowing our center of gravity to glide around over our base of support.

Not releasing our legs from the very top of the thigh as the horse's motion lifts your platform will show up quickly, the faster and bigger the horse's strides. Gripping does work up to the point your own muscle power can overcome the horse's movement, but no further. It can then seem best to hold the horse's motion down to the level you can outmuscle, until the horse's movement becomes a resource rather than a problem. How big and quick a stride you can accept from the horse is a good indicator of how well you use the horse's motion to your advantage.

Our platform must also be arranged with one seatbone, one shoulder, and one ear on either side of the horse's spine, or the lifting motion of the horse's back will swing our platform and even our whole torso sideward rather than upward. That can also make us feel we need to grip with our legs to stay stable. It will also swing our weight more to one side, making it difficult for the horse to move straightly and for the rider to keep both stirrups equally easily.

Lift can come from the hind leg action being transmitted through the horse's barrel to the forehand, as we just discussed. It can also come from the phases of suspension when the hooves are all in the air, part of most gaits' normal footfall pattern, although not the walk (see Chapter 4). However the lift happens, we want to allow the horse its full range of back motion and its full phase of suspension, so as not to disconnect its hindquarters from its forehand.

It's a contradiction to ask the horse to do things that would normally create lift, and then interfere with movement because of our rigidity. If we force the horse to move out even though we clench on its back, a logical horse, feeling its back in something like a vise grip, might conclude we want its legs to move more, but not its back. We may well teach the horse to become a "leg-goer"—legs flinging around like all get-out, but its back relatively immobile. That is not the kind of movement that makes an athlete, and it's hard on horses' backs and hocks to move that way. As we have seen, partial success can be very compelling. More leg action with incomplete back activity, what I call "Barishnikov in a straitjacket," may look flashy at least in terms of leg action, even though we haven't really allowed the horse its full range of motion. Leg-goers are also about as comfortable to ride as a square-wheeled bicycle.

Sitting a horse that has a mobile, supple back is like riding a wave. A horse with a well-developed, active back is a dream to sit even at full extended trot. Supple springiness in all limbs and the horse's back greatly moderates the concussion when the horse's feet return to the ground. In fact, a rough-gaited horse can be made much easier to sit by first suppling its back to develop its full range of motion and then strengthening it. A springy back can cushion the gaits for horse and rider both.

We can use the lift to communicate how much movement we will accept from the horse's back, and therefore from its hindquarters. Staying light in the saddle at the top of the back's upward swing can suggest that we would be happy to give the horse more room to move. Prolonging the lift can suggest that the horse is welcome to take some extra time in its steps. This is good if we want bigger steps, since big, high, or long steps take more time than cramped steps.

Our weight has to go somewhere if it lightens in the saddle, and gravity will automatically drop it to our stirrups if we let it. Letting the lift in the horse's motion lighten our platform in the saddle goes along with letting our legs slip down the horse's sides. As we allow our seat to lighten in the saddle, we can let our contact area lengthen and our stirrup connection improve, too. The horse can definitely feel our weight ease on its back and our legs lengthen along its sides. Some people call that "the seat aid creating the leg aid." Using the platform and contact area in harmony like this makes much more sense than trying to use either our platform or seat, but not both in harmony, to communicate to the horse.

The horse's motion can start our platform into an even more distinct upward and forward motion, if we let it. Our center of gravity can swing quite a bit upward and forward and still be well within our base of support. We can let our platform drift quite a bit away from the saddle and yet stay securely connected with the horse through our contact area and stirrups. This can be even more secure than sitting heavily and tightly in the saddle without letting our legs drop toward the stirrups. We can allow our platform to drift up and forward out of the saddle when it is more work to oppose the gait's lift and swing than to let our platform float for a bit. Some people call that posting, or rising to the trot.

Rising works at the canter, too, allowing our platform to drift away from the saddle every other stride. It is very comfortable, unlike just bumping in the saddle every stride. You may well see riders who canter a lot use it the most. Many foxhunters, jump riders, cowboys, and polo players use this strategy.

Going Down?

Let's look at how we can use the drop in a horse's back to become more secure and comfortable and to communicate with the horse.

What part of the horse's movement drops your platform? As in the previous experiment, simply note these moments, saying "now" every time you feel the horse's back dropping.

If your platform is rather immobile, you can identify the drop through momentary decreases in pressure under one or both seatbones. It feels like the horse is dropping away from your seatbone(s), which is exactly what is happening. There might be a momentary and perhaps repeating void between the saddle and your platform, or one side of it, or one side and then the other.

If your platform is generally in contact with the saddle because your spine flexes as the horse's back drops, you'll get much the same feel as when your spine flexed to accommodate the lift: your platform rolling in the saddle, shifting along the length of your seatbones, or sliding along the skin between the seatbones and the saddle. You will feel your waist flexing, and maybe sense your rib cage dropping and lifting.

Your platform can rest quietly in the saddle when your spine is stable and your weight falls over consistent points of your platform, while your hip joints and leg joints absorb the horse's movements. You can identify when the horse's movement is dropping your platform because the drop closes the angles between your upper body and thighs, the angles between your thighs and knees, and the angles between your shins and the top of your feet. It would be like standing on the ground with your knees somewhat bent and allowing someone to push one or both seatbones lower. Note that a springy rebound easily follows this momentary compression, if you let it.

Just like in the lifting phase, most of the action is between the rider's torso and the thighs (in the hip joints), between the thighs and the shins (in the knees), and between the shins and feet (ankles), rather than from a wavy spine. The drop of the horse's back flexes our leg joints and asks our legs to operate like springs, not rigid columns.

The moment when our platform sinks toward our feet is obviously a good moment to let our weight drop into the stirrups. Let your torso/thigh, thigh/shin, and shin/foot angles close softly as your platform drops and voila! your contact area stays nicely low on the horse's sides. Your horse's downward motion can help drop your knees right down into the sweet spots of the saddle, and your weight can travel from there on down to the stirrups. It will slip down anyway just by gravity, if you let it. Why fight it, since that's what we want?

The drop (and the lift) can also be a great time to take some pressure off your hip, knees, or ankles if you have been bracing them. You can use the opening/closing action of the horse's lift and drop almost like mini-massages for your joints, rather than subjecting them to the jar and compression of riding with stiff, propped legs. Luckily, that will create a more consistent connection with your horse, with all the benefits that provides.

Using the Drop for Security and Communication

This dropping motion of the horse's back can help us become more secure and comfortable on a horse a few ways. If we let it, the horse's motion will shift our platform and contact area into a downward and forward motion with no effort on our part, just by letting gravity do its job. Whenever you want to connect more with the saddle and the stirrups, it is literally as easy as dropping onto a trampoline.

The same things have to be true to use this phase of the gaits to drop your weight into the stirrups as for the lifting phase. You have to be very accommodating around the tops of your thighs. All limb joints must be in free play, although in this case they need to be free to close rather than open. Your platform has to be arranged with one seatbone, shoulder, and ear on either side of the horse's spine.

You might want to let the horse's back drop away from your platform if your horse has a tight or tender back. Rather than pushing away from the horse's back to get a softer platform connection, we can just let it drop away from our platform, if we want the horse to experience less contact on its back from the rider. As the horse gains trust that it will be allowed to move its back without disturbance, its back can start to supple and strengthen, which will make all of its work easier and more athletic.

Using the drop to lower our platform and contact area can help maintain or even amplify our contact area's connection with the horse's barrel, if that is what we want the horse to experience. Bonus question: what would that likely convey to the horse?

You can use the drop to start you downward if you do want to drop rather heavily on the horse's back, but pushing down on a horse's back is akin to someone digging knuckles into your back. Horses tend to tighten and withdrawn their backs from this kind of treatment, just like people do. I can't think of too many times we want to do that on purpose, but it's available if you need it.

We can also prolong the drop just enough to suggest we would be happy to give the horse more time to take longer, more sweeping, higher or slower steps. We don't want to confuse hastiness with more athletic movement.

Allowing the horse's motion to move us this way makes more sense than holding our legs rigidly on either side of the horse, with the horse's barrel bumping up against them, left and right, as it tries to do its job. A logical horse could either assume these bumps felt a lot like legs aids and go faster, or it could learn that wasn't what we wanted after all if we tug on reins and thump on backs. It could then logically assume legs aids don't count unless they are much stronger. Or, it could figure we want it to hold its barrel still while its legs move more. That's a leg-goer in the works again, instead of a horse whose topline is at least unhindered.

Going Right or Left?

There is a left/right emphasis to the horse's lift and drop, but there is more left/right motion in the horse's barrel than in its topline. The barrel's left/right swing is going to influence our contact area more than our platform. The lift and drop of the top of the horse's back most directly influences our platform, while the left/right swing of the horse's barrel most directly influences our contact area.

We saw that the horse's back is highest when the hind legs are passing each other directly under the horse's pelvis at the walk, with one hind leg in support and one in flight. The horse's back is lowest when the hind legs are farthest apart from each other, one touching down forward under the horse's belly and the other pushing off behind the horse's body. We can identify these phases of the walk by whether the horse is lifting or dropping our platform.

We get even more specific about what the horse is doing with its hind legs by using our contact area, too. Try this:

Use a mirror if you have one, or a keen-eyed observer if you have one of those, or a video camera, or all of them. One thing you will need for sure is a wide-open sensory system. Walk around saying "left" out loud every time you feel the left side of the horse's barrel swinging from left to right when it has reached as far to the right as it goes. What is the horse's left hind leg doing at the moment you are saying "left"? Is it in the support phase, swinging back to push off, lifting off the ground, folding and swinging forward, extending forward to touch down, or already touched down and moving into the support phase again? Take your time to observe this carefully, and make a note of what you find out.

Next, the right side of the horse. Walk around saying "right" out loud every time you feel the right side of the horse's barrel swinging from the right toward the left when it has reached as far to the left as it is going to go. What is the horse's right hind leg doing at the moment you are saying "right"? Make a note of that.

The next step, of course, is to call both "left" and "right" as each side of the horse's barrel swings back and forth. If you are perfectly honest about reporting what you feel, you might well find yourself going along like this: "left, right, left, right, left, what? left, uh, left, nothing, nothing, right, oops, I'm going the wrong way, right, right? That can't be, lost it." This is excellent. It is much more telling than just assuming the horse has maintained a consistent stride, which is rather unlikely. So, just keep talking, loud and clear.

It is common during this experiment for riders to kind of tighten down a little to try to feel the horse's motion more clearly. Not surprising, horses tend to either jig or slow down. The horse's responses to how it experiences being ridden are always of interest, but what matters for this experiment is that you keep saying "left," "right," or "now" or something every time the horse swings its barrel.

Some riders try to get with this left/right swing by shifting or even shoving their platform from side to side. The tricky part about that is that our seatbones could feel very still in the saddle even when the saddle is getting shoved across the horse's back. This is obviously using too many muscles, imposing a motion rather than taking it from the horse and not letting your hip joints play freely in their sockets. Remember, the left/right swing is more noticeable lower down the horse's rib cage, where the rider's knees or perhaps calves connect with the horse. There is minimal left-right swing along the horse's topline, where our platform is, compared with lower down the horse's side, where our contact area is.

Putting the lift/drop and the left/right swing together can tell us very precisely what the horse is doing. The horse's barrel swings away from each hind leg as it advances in its flight phase, and swings toward whichever hind leg is taking over the support phase. So, although it isn't exactly accurate, many riders pick this up most easily by thinking of the horse getting its barrel out of the way as a hind leg swings forward.

If you want to get really technical, we see that at the walk:

We can tell the left hind leg is:	When the horse's back:	And the barrel is:
Reaching farthest forward to touch down	Drops	Swinging to the right, as if the horse is getting its barrel out of the way of the advancing left hindleg
In its support phase	Lifts	Swinging left toward the supporting left hindleg
Moving into its push-off phase	Drops	Swinging farthest to the left
In its flight phase	Lifts	Swinging right, toward the supporting right hindleg

So, the lift/drop of our platform plus the left/right of our contact area tells us quite precisely what each of the horse's hind legs are doing. Since the hind legs' action is the source of everything we want to do with a horse, this is fundamentally useful information. It may seem impossible right now to sort this all out enough for practical use. For the moment, it is quite sufficient to know that it is possible to become this familiar with your horse's movement at the walk and at the other gaits, too.

If you want to check this back motion/phase of the step connection, it's easy enough. Lead an unsaddled horse around (a walk is fine) with your hand flat on the horse's back about where your seatbone would be. First just check how you can tell when the horse's back is lifting or dropping, and then observe where the same-side hind leg is as the horse's back lifts. Is it directly under the stifle? Swinging back? Fully extended backward? Lifting? Folding and swinging forward? Touching down? Starting to move backward to accept weight?

Check the patterns when the horse's back is dropping. Notice the other parts of the horse's back, farther back toward its loins and farther forward toward the withers. Does checking different areas along the horse's back change things? What does that tell you about how the horse's hind leg action travels forward along the horse's spine? Since that's what we are sitting on, that would be a good thing to know.

Check the motion all along the horse's topline and barrel. The spine and pelvis may move in relation to each other in ways we might not have expected, but it is easy enough to find out.

Bonus question: What happens farther down the horse's rib cage, about where your knee or calf would be? How is the horse's barrel swinging at each phase of the action of the hind leg on that side? Up? Down? Toward the same side hind leg or away from it?

Using the Left/Right Swing

Our timing when we apply aids can make a tremendous difference in the message we convey to the horse. For example, if you use a left leg aid when the horse's left hind leg is pushing off, you are asking for increased push-off from the left hind leg. If you use a left leg aid when the horse's left hind leg is swinging forward, you are asking for more forward swing from the left hind leg. "So what?" you may ask.

Try it yourself. Walk along a bit and see what happens when you swing one leg more forward versus pushing off more with one leg. Try both methods with each leg, and you might be surprised. Both will result in a bigger step, but no doubt we each find it easier to reach with one leg and to push with the other. One method probably creates a bigger step more easily than the other. It would not be at all unusual for one way to feel quite normal but to have to really think about how to go about things the other way. Depending on our holding patterns, our upper body may well operate differently in one case than the other, too.

It's the same for horses. They are born with certain preferences and dexterities, like people are right-handed or left-handed. They can also develop postural habits, like people. These asymmetries and localized tensions or weaknesses have far-reaching consequences for our horse's performance and long-term soundness. Our riding can confirm these limitations to the horses performance, add new ones . . . or resolve them.

It is going to be naturally easier for the horse to respond to our request to reach more forward with one hind leg than the other. It will be easier for the horse to respond to our request to push off with one hind leg than the other. In other words, the horse is going to respond to some of our aids more promptly and accurately than others.

The horse will also handle some physical demands more easily than others. For example, a horse who doesn't have much forward reach from its left hind is going to handle a left turn toward a five-foot (or a five-inch) jump differently than it handles a right turn toward that jump. One hind leg is going to support and push the horse's body differently than the other hind leg. The gymnastic effort is going to be very different than it would be for a horse that has developed the reach, support, and push skills more equally in both hind legs.

A horse that lacks push-off power on one hind leg has different physical issues than one which lacks forward swing in that leg. It's different again for a horse that doesn't have much scope in general. Differences in the habitual use of each hind leg will certainly influence the muscle play throughout the horse's entire body and will show up throughout a horse's performance in any sport, and ultimately affect its soundness. You probably already sense that your horse responds better to some aids and demands than to others. This may help explain why that is. Whether you activate a reach or a push will also make a difference, especially in transitions, as we will see.

All horse sports call on the reach and push of both hind legs in both directions, so all sports benefit from equalizing the horse's hind leg strength and dexterity and how that travels through the rest of their body.

Like people, horses will tend to use their strengths and protect their weaknesses. That means the strong parts tend to get overused before the weak parts get called on to help. It is a shame to see a horse made useless (lame) by habitually overusing one hock, before the other one was called on to help. Symmetrical gymnastic development can have very practical consequences for your horse's tendons and joints and its physical ability to respond to our aids and meet all of our demands equally well. That can have obvious safety consequences.

As our horses' gym teachers, we go about things differently when we know our horse has a harder time reaching with its left hind leg than with its right hind leg, for example. You would want your gym teacher to help you improve your particular weaknesses before they put you to serious work; I believe we should do no less for our horses.

I really get a kick out of people who spend time teaching their horse stuff on the ground, but don't seem to apply what they learned to saddle time. I've seen any number of people who easily taught their horse to lower its head from a slight pressure on its poll. It rarely takes half an hour for that to be in pretty good order.

What I find intriguing is that not nearly as many of those same people (and a lot of other folks who don't get into groundwork as much) have also gotten their horse to respond well to leg aids. Folks who have proved they can teach a horse to respond well to pressure under one circumstance may not accomplish basically the same thing under saddle, where it really counts.

How can a person teach one thing so easily in one case and not teach it just as easily in the other? What are people doing that works very well in one case, but they aren't doing in the other case? Why does the horse get such a different message in one case than the other?

Riding Without Stirrups

How our weight is transmitted to the ground as we stand and walk says much about our overall alignment and balance on the ground. Similarly, how our weight is transmitted to the stirrups says much about our balance, flexibility, and symmetry when we are mounted.

Riding without stirrups can develop a sense of riding the horse instead of the equipment. Once riders have the experience that the essence of their security lies in fluidity and harmony among their platform, contact area, and the horse's movement, their legs usually relax out of their death grip on the saddle. Their legs can then just maintain a nice, consistent connection with the horse. As their legs lengthen easily from the top of the thighs, their contact area drops considerably and their stirrup connection improves or they can ride easily with longer stirrups without reducing the weight that lands in them. Should a real need for gripping arise, it will be that much more effective with the contact area lower on the horse's sides.

Riding without stirrups may give a rider confidence that they can stay on even if they lose a stirrup or both of them. It may help a rider discover that balance, suppleness, and attention to their interface with the horse works better than prolonged gripping. This discovery may only come after sheer exhaustion of the leg muscles. That is an unnecessarily hard way to open the door to correct use of the stirrups.

Riding without stirrups may teach a rider many things, but it cannot teach a rider how to use the stirrups well. Stirrups at the correct length catch the weight we allow to drop into them, hold the rider's toes up for them, support the rider's legs, and impart the desired knee angle.

Instead of supporting the rider's legs and catching their weight, stirrups can feel to some riders like they are pushing the rider's leg upward or cramping a rider's ankles, knees, and hips into certain angles. This can easily promote gripping upwards, away from the stirrups, to stay on. Riders who use upward grip often prefer riding without stirrups. Since their legs are consistently pulling upwards away from the stirrups, they lose them frequently and would just as soon do without them. It is not uncommon for such riders to leave their knees high and to push on their stirrups from the knee down, or to push on or grip the stirrups with their toes. They may have strong legs, but not much weight in the stirrup. If the stirrup is removed, such riders' legs often don't change at all even if the stirrup was rather short. If a rider is truly open and released throughout their platform and contact area, their whole leg will drop down of its own weight if the stirrup is removed. If that doesn't happen, something other than the stirrup is holding the rider's legs up and preventing gravity from dropping them down the horse's side. What could that be but the rider's own muscles?

Riding without stirrups may well just confirm habits instead of developing a better use of stirrups. Letting the stirrups go can be a tremendous relief, especially on some riders' cramped knees and ankles, until riders experience the benefits of releasing their muscles while they use stirrups, too.

Work without stirrups can deeply convince some riders that gripping, especially gripping upward, is the primary way to stay on the horse. This is especially true if riders are asked to do things without stirrups for which their

A strong leg, seemingly in good position, but where is this rider's weight likely to land in the next split second?

A more likely way to make the horse's job easier.

freedom of motion is not yet developed enough to do well. Very basic grab reflexes kick in when a rider loses balance and consistent interface with the horse, and the rider learns (likely without knowing they learned it) that gripping works. Gripping does work, but only to the extent that we really can physically overpower the movement of an animal that outweighs us by a factor of about ten. That isn't very far.

This easily leads to the vicious circle in which the rider is very motivated to keep the horse's movement below the level they can overcome by muscle. In their heart of hearts, they know that they do not have sufficient balance and mobility to adapt to larger movement from the horse, and that their muscle power isn't sufficient, either. Far better to use work without stirrups very judiciously to develop the rider's sense of balance and suppleness before getting into situations where resorting to gripping up into the saddle can seem like the best choice.

Riding without stirrups does make it impossible for a rider to push their platform away from the horse by pushing on the stirrups, and that can help a rider get a sense of what a better platform connection and supple leg connection are like. Riding bareback is great to get a sense of whether you have one seatbone on either side of the horse's spine, and of how many back muscles the horse uses. Riding without stirrups may help if it doesn't develop even more tension. It may also help a rider learn to use the horse's motion to create a smooth, perfectly timed posting trot that comes from allowing the lift to open the appropriate angles. Posting without stirrups is often used instead to strengthen a rider's leg grip.

A well-balanced, symmetrical, and supple rider can perform equally well with stirrups or without them, or with only one stirrup. That is the true test of how well a rider relates to their horse and their stirrups. That is different than feeling secure only with or only without both stirrups.

A short safety note: if you are pretty sure you are about to fall off, get your feet out of your stirrups ASAP, to avoid getting a foot trapped in a stirrup and being dragged after the fall. Get very familiar with the emergency dismount and practice it regularly when other people are around, especially if your horse is not accustomed to it.

What about the Other Gaits?

Once you've got the general idea of using the lifting, dropping, and swinging movements to improve your seat and communication at the walk, you can use the same principles at the other gaits. We will learn much more about all of the horse's gaits in the next chapter, but you have the skills now to explore how to use each of the gaits to improve your own seat according to your own build. It all comes down to the lift, drop, and swing in the rhythm of any gait.

The gaits that include phases of suspension do change things somewhat. The lift and drop at the walk come only from the extension and flexion of the legs since the walk always has two or three feet on the ground. At the trot, canter, and gallop, some additional lift comes from the horse pushing its entire body off the ground, called a phase of suspension. Still, a lift is a lift, a drop is a drop, and a swing is a swing whether it comes more from the horse's hind leg action traveling forward along the horse's spine, as in the walk, or more from the horse's entire body lifting off the ground and descending again, as in the trot, canter, and gallop. Each of the gaits will be discussed in greater detail, but I encourage you to explore how to use the lift, drop, and left/right swing of each of the gaits as you explored them at the walk.

The lift of the horse's entire body at the trot is much more evident than the lift of the horse's back at the walk, as you can see in the silhouette illustration of the trot. Compare it to the illustration of the walk. You have to be medium sensitive to identify the back's lifting actions at the walk; you're not likely to miss the lift of the horse's whole body during phases of suspension at the trot. The two left/right swings of the rib cage per stride may not be as obvious in the trot as at the walk, but they are there. The trot is rather like a trampoline. You can let it launch you or you can soften its lift according to how softly you use your legs and how your center of gravity lines up with your base of support.

The rocking-horse motion of the canter may be more obvious than the left/right swing of the barrel, but one swing per stride is there, too. The canter's three-beat, rocking-horse action gives a different feel of the horse's hind leg action. The horse's forehand will be higher during the first beat of the canter, when one hind leg is on the ground and both forelegs are in flight.

The horse's withers and hips don't oscillate in relation to each other as much in the trot as they do in the walk and canter. Instead, the horse tends to lift as a whole in the trot's phase of suspension and drop the most when the horse's legs are bearing maximum weight. The pasterns, shoulders, hocks, stifles, and hips all flex to absorb the impact of the horse hitting the ground.

We can see the rocking-chair action as the horse progresses from the first beat of a canter stride to the last beat. The forehand is higher as each canter stride begins, and the hind-quarters are higher as each stride ends.

The horse's body is more or less horizontal in the second beat, and the horse's hindquarters are relatively high in the third beat, when the horse only has one foreleg on the ground. You can see this in the silhouette illustrations of the canter.

The canter is rather like a teeter-totter. Let your joint angles close and your platform drift toward the stirrups as the horse's back drops away from your seat in the first beat of the canter, like you would when your side of the teeter-totter is going down. Let them open and let your platform move away from the stirrups as the horse's back end lifts in the second and third beat of the canter, as you would when your side of the teeter-totter is going up. This will leave your platform nicely in contact with the saddle for all three beats and the phase of suspension of this gait, too.

If the rider stays away from the horse's back in any of the gaits, as in some two-point or jumping positions, the hind leg action can be felt as the saddle approaches and then falls away from the rider's platform. Or, the rider can simply stay a bit more on the area in front of the seatbones, in what has been called a light seat or a half-seat, or sometimes a forward seat.

We can use every phase of every step of every gait to let the horse's motion give us more security in the saddle and the stirrups. When we use the horse's motion as a resource, the bigger the horse moves, the better we sit and the better and more consistent our stirrup connection gets. We can also use the horse's motion to tell quite accurately what the horse's hind legs are doing, so we can use the horse's motion to offer us excellent timing for our aids.

We will find that the horse's motion itself will virtually hand us perfect timing for our aids on a silver platter, if we let it. Changing from one gait to another is often no more than adjusting the action of one or two of the horse's legs at a certain time. Knowing there is a moment when it is easier to activate or delay a leg to get a certain result will tend to make you more sensitive to those moments. Just knowing the possibility exists is sufficient for the time being.

As we next explore in some detail each of the four gaits, keep in mind how you have used and will in the future use the horse's motion.

CHAPTER 4

How Horses Move

Allah took the wind and made the horse.
—Anonymous

There is something about the outside of a horse that is good for a man.
—Sir Winston Churchill

To make oneself understood is certainly impossible without far-reaching comprehension of the other's standpoint.
—CG Jung

To use the horse's motion well for security, and to use it well to communicate what we want the horse to do, we need to know:

1. What the horse is doing;
2. How that needs to be changed, if at all;
3. How to convey that to the horse; and,
4. Whether it happened.

In other words, to be fair gym teachers and religion teachers to our horses, we need to know about the horse's gait mechanics. The better we understand the horse's movement, the more easily we can communicate how we want it to change. We can consistently know whether we got what we wanted or not and therefore more accurately shape the horse's behavior. You know now how to find out what the horse is doing, so you could figure this all out on your own. Consider this chapter a cheat sheet for some of what you could dis-cover on your own about each gait and its advantages and disadvantages.

All four-legged animals move the same way. Muscles far above the legs move the limbs. Tendons and ligaments transmit the action to the lower joints, right on down to the hooves or feet. The bones move as allowed by the design of the joints, ligaments, and tendons.

The forelegs, operated primarily by muscles in and around the shoulder and the neck, are built like support columns. They mainly support rather than add much push or pull to the stride. Forelegs can pull the body forward some-what, especially for climbing, but they basically support the weight pushed there by the hind legs. What the forelegs do largely depends on what the hind legs do, rather than the other way around.

Starting from the moment when the hind foot is directly under the hip and bearing the most weight, muscles in the pelvis and upper hind leg rotate the limb backward, which propels the horse's body forward. The hind leg pushes off, lifts, flexes, swings forward, straightens, touches down, and starts its backward rotation into the support phase again.

The spine and trunk transmit the hind legs' thrust toward the forehand. Think of the horse's center of gravity as a little bag of water suspended within the rib cage from the spine, somewhat behind the horse's shoulders and above the elbows. As a hind leg pushes the body forward, the bag of water/center of gravity swings forward and somewhat sideward. A foreleg touches down to catch that weight. The other hind leg does its thing, the bag sloshes forward and a bit the other way, and the other foreleg touches down to catch that swing.

So, the bag of water/center of gravity swings within the horse's rib cage according to how the hind legs operate and how that action is transmitted forward along the horse's spine. The forelegs respond as necessary. In fact, what the forelegs are doing is a good indicator of what the horse's center of gravity is doing.

If the horse's hind legs operate consistently and the spine transmits that action accurately, the bag of water/center of gravity swings consistently. If a hind leg changes how it operates, or if the spine transmits that action differ-ently, the swing changes and the foreleg changes its operation, too. Something about the horse's alignment, orientation, or line of travel will change, too, unless we interfere with the horse's normal mechanisms.

The head and neck participate in movement, too. They may move to express the horse's emotions, help maintain or restore balance, or gather sensory information, but the head and neck don't initiate motion. The hind legs and back have the majority vote about everything the horse does.

It makes a big difference if you ask a horse to activate a hind leg during the flight, support, or push-off phase, as you would end up doing different things if someone asked you to put more power in your step when your leg was on the ground, in the air, swinging forward, or swinging backward. A horse might easily respond to a badly timed aid by doing something other than what you thought you asked it to do. So, clear communication with horses is easier when you understand their gaits clearly. You can ask the horse to do what you want it to do most easily when you understand how the horse gets its side of the job done.

The footfall (the order in which each foot touches down) and the phases (which feet are on the ground) in each of these gaits is as follows. We will start with the outside hind in each gait for ease of discussion.

THE WALK

The walk is a four-beat gait with this footfall:
1. Outside hind
2. Outside fore
3. Inside hind
4. Inside fore

Each foot lands independently at the walk, so four feet equals four beats. The walk has eight phases, or eight different ways the horse's feet support the horse's weight:
1. Inside hind and inside fore (outside fore just lifted)
2. Inside hind, inside fore, and outside hind (outside hind touches down as the first beat)

3. Inside fore and outside hind (inside hind has lifted)

4. Inside fore, outside hind, and outside fore (outside fore touches down as the second beat)

5. Outside hind and outside fore (inside fore has lifted)

6. Outside hind, outside fore, and inside hind (inside hind touches down as the third beat)

7. Outside fore and inside hind (outside hind has lifted)

8. Outside fore, inside hind, and inside fore (inside fore touches down as the fourth beat)

The walk is unique in a few ways. It is the only gait with no phase of suspension. The horse always has two or three legs on the ground, so the horse is least likely to lose its balance at the walk. On the other hand, the horse can most easily resist the rider at the walk, since the horse can resist most effectively when its feet are on the ground.

The walk is also a relatively lazy gait for many horses, so it is easy to lose forwardness, that wonderful sense of wanting to get somewhere. This loss of forwardness can be harder to detect at the walk than at the other gaits. Because of these tendencies, nothing seemingly complicated happens at a walk until second level dressage work, for example, which is fairly far along.

On the plus side, the walk can have a calming effect on the horse (or is it just dulled with boredom?), which can be helpful. It may be a good warm-up gait and is useful for cooling a horse out. Most riders can sit a walk, more or less, so it can be useful to sort some things out in a kind of slow motion. Still, the walk is more useful to teach the rider some things than it is for gymnasticizing a horse very much. As the saying goes, the trot prepares the horse for the canter, and the canter develops the walk. We'll see more about why that is as we go along.

Deterioration of the quality of the walk is a sure sign something is going wrong in the training as a whole. The only movement that is in every dressage test from pre-training up through Grand Prix is the free walk on a long rein. An upper-level rider who wants to wow a judge in a Grand Prix test will show a really good free walk on a long rein without any neck, leg, or back constriction before, during, or after that movement.

The most common fault of the correctness of the footfall at the walk is a pacey walk, sometimes called a camel walk, in which the lateral pairs of legs touch down almost at the same time instead of in distinctly separated beats. This makes a walk rhythm of 1, 2 . . . 3, 4, instead of a clear, even beat for each foot: 1, 2, 3, 4. This is usually a symptom of a foreleg touching down earlier than it otherwise would, probably because a foreleg is carrying more weight than it usually does. The hind leg may have been slowed or didn't move far enough forward to help carry the horse's weight. Often, this is a sign of back problems.

Another common gait fault at the walk is jigging, when the horse tosses in a few trot-like steps here and there. This could be a little *joie de vivre*, a sign of anxiety or eagerness, or trained in to show the judge or spectators how spirited the horse is or what brave riders we are. Letting your horse jig may come back to haunt you when you start work on piaffe and passage, but you can't say playing around like that isn't fun for horse and rider. If you are going to jig for fun, please at least do it with an even rhythm.

The walk has variations that are natural or taught to horses, such as running walks, ambles, or singlefoot. Any horse might throw in a couple ambly-like strides here and there, and some breeds have a talent for these specialty gaits that can be developed to a high expertise, which is hardly a fault of gait. The Spanish Walk is not natural to the horse, or at least I have never seen a horse volunteer the Spanish Walk (as opposed to striking a few times in a row) at liberty, but it is showy and may have some gymnastic benefits.

THE TROT

The trot is a two-beat gait with two phases of suspension, with this footfall:
1. Outside hind and inside fore together (inside hind and outside fore in flight)
2. Phase of suspension
3. Inside hind and outside fore together (outside hind and inside fore in flight)
4. Phase of suspension

At the trot, the horse jumps from one diagonal pair of legs to the other, each beat separated by a phase of suspension in which all feet are in flight. The phases of the trot are the same as the footfall of the trot. The trot and the pace are the only forward-moving gaits in which the footfall is the same as the phases.

The pace is also a two-beat gait, but the pace uses lateral pairs of legs instead of diagonal pairs. At the pace, the outside hind and the outside fore touch down together followed by a phase of suspension, and then the inside hind and inside fore touch down together, followed by another phase of suspension. The pace isn't used much under saddle so we won't discuss it further, but good harness racers use the pace to achieve speeds some galloping Thoroughbreds only wish they could manage on their best day.

The trot is inherently a little more energetic than a walk, perhaps because some degree of push is required to lift the horse off the ground in the phases of suspension, however fleeting that phase may be. Since the horse can most easily unbalance during phases of suspension, the trot may be somewhat less stable than the walk.

On the other hand, the phase of suspension is often the easiest moment to influence the horse, for better or worse. Just as a swinging pendulum is easier to move than a weight lying on your carpet, a horse is less able to resist the rider's influence in the phase of suspension than when its feet are on the ground. Not incapable, just less so. We have two such phases in every trot stride, and we are wise to make good use of them gymnastically and diagnostically.

The trot and pace are also the only symmetrical forward-moving gaits. What one side of the horse's body does in one beat will be mirrored by the other side of its body in the next beat. This makes the trot, in all its variations—including the tempi (lengths of stride) and two-track movements, plus piaffe and passage—a relatively easy gait at which to see how one side of the horse's body compares with the other side. You might even hear the diagonal footfalls as ONE, two, ONE, two instead of one, two, one, two. Inequality in the diagonal pairs of legs at any kind of trot points clearly to asymmetrical strength and dexterity or rider imbalance. Certainly the trot offers the easiest way to diagnose whether your work is developing the horse as you hoped, since it will most clearly show whether the horse is developing symmetrically.

This symmetry of gait at the trot also means that we can focus the gymnastic effect of some exercises on a particular part of the horse more easily at the trot than at the other gaits. Focusing gymnastic efforts on particular areas can be done at the other gaits, and each gait has certain gymnastic advantages, but it is often easiest at the trot. For example, if you decide that the left hind lacks a bit of swing, working a horse correctly with the left hind on the outside of the circle could help. A well-ridden circle can influence the horse to naturally add a little more swing to that left hind simply because the outside legs may follow a slightly longer path than the inside legs do.

Given the trot's somewhat higher inherent energy level, its two phases of suspension, and its symmetry, the trot is the gait of choice for much of our gymnastisizing work.

The diagonal pair of feet take off and land at the same time if the center of gravity is equally well supported by the hind legs and the forelegs. A quick study of horse magazines photos will clearly show pictures of trots with a hind foot lifting off before the diagonal fore foot has done so. You can also tell where the horse's weight is being supported by how deeply the pasterns are flexed. A forefoot that stays on the ground longer than a hind leg or that has a more deeply flexed pastern than a hind leg shows that the center of gravity is somewhat more toward the forehand than the hindquarters. That often goes along with overflexion in the neck. Look at some harness racing trotter photos, though, and you will likely see the opposite—a hind leg touching down well before the diagonal foreleg touches the ground.

Loss of suspension at any gait or speed generally indicates a lack of suppleness and dexterity. The horse may have decided it is a good idea to reduce the phase of suspension until the rider can balance better, or it may reduce the phase of suspension if its tack or shoes are uncomfortable, for example. Horses that were having a grand time floating around the field fifteen minutes ago with nary a hoof touched to ground may seem incapable of heaving its hulk two inches into the air under saddle. On the other hand, a horse whose center of gravity swings steadily will feel a greater freedom in its leg play and will often volunteer a longer phase of suspension. A horse without much suspension goes faster by quickening its strides, not by using air time. Hastiness is not a sign of the dexterity and free movement that make for athleticism. If the phase of suspension is minimal or gone, one must ask: why is a horse less willing or able to lift itself off the ground under saddle than it would at liberty? How can we recapture under saddle the ability the horse shows at liberty?

THE CANTER

The canter is a three-beat gait with one phase of suspension, with this footfall:

1. Outside hind
2. Inside hind and outside fore together
3. Inside fore
4. Phase of suspension

The canter is an interesting gait, especially regarding its six phases.

1. Outside hind (first beat, three legs in flight)
2. Outside hind, inside hind, and outside fore (diagonal pair touches down as second beat, inside fore in flight)
3. Inside hind and outside fore (outside hind has lifted)
4. Inside hind, outside fore, and inside fore (inside fore touches down as the third beat)
5. Inside fore (inside hind and outside fore have lifted)
6. Phase of suspension (inside fore has lifted, all feet in the air)

The canter also has leads, unlike the walk or trot. That is to say, the canter footfall can begin with the left hind leg, move over to the diagonal pair of right hind and left fore, and end with the right fore—a canter on the right lead. Or the canter can begin with the right hind leg, move over to the diagonal of the left hind and right fore, and end with the left fore—a canter on the left lead. Although a canter is said to be a left lead or a right lead canter, what we call the leading leg is actually the last leg to hit the ground. It does look like the leading leg is ahead of the other legs, so many riders are surprised to learn the leading leg is the last beat of a canter stride.

The canter is inherently livelier and something horses often do at play, so it might wake up a lazy or bored horse. The canter is the gait of choice for many horses, especially Thoroughbreds with expertise at that gait fairly singing in their blood. A lively canter may be somewhat more prone to loss of balance than the trot or walk because of its liveliness and its single, more pro- longed phase of suspension.

Many older or lazy horses prefer a tight little canter to a bigger, freer trot. The canter offers support from three feet on the ground to ease legs that are getting creaky.

The canter and canter transitions work the lumbar-sacral area between the saddle and the horse's pelvis in ways no other gait or transition quite man- ages. The footfall sequence also means the inside hip and shoulder work more to the fore of the outside hip and shoulder, so canter work can relatively stretch the muscles on the outside of the horse. So, if you want to stretch the left side of the horse's back, good quality canter work on the right lead is one of several tools to get you there. The canter can also develop the horse's abdominal muscles that help draw the hind legs forward. If you want to work a hay belly down, good canter work will do that faster than trot work.

We generally canter on the inside lead, so cantering on the outside lead is said to be wrong, at least until we start doing it on purpose. Then, a canter on the outside lead, called a counter-canter, is considered a rather advanced movement. A correct counter-canter is a great way to develop the forward reach of the hind leg on the leading side. The real question is whether we are getting the lead we intend to get. If not, why not?

The main fault of correctness of footfall at the canter is the always-faulty four-beat canter, in which the outside fore lands before the inside hind dur- ing the second beat. The inside hind leg must have been restricted from com- ing forward far enough or fast enough to synchronize with the outside fore. The outside foreleg must then touch down early to support the weight the horse didn't catch with the hind leg.

The other fault of footfall at the canter is cross-cantering, also called cantering disunited, in which the forelegs are on one lead and the hind legs are on the other. Cross-cantering usually happens when the forelegs switch leads a few strides before the hind legs do so. Cross-cantering can be a sign of back stiffness, or at least that the horse's spine has not adopted the same curvature throughout its length for a few strides. That may be an inefficient use of the hindquarters' power to push the horse directly forward, so it is not considered desirable. Flying changes of lead with both ends changing within one stride seem to demonstrate a more supple, symmetrical, and ambidextrous horse.

It is not uncommon to see horses at liberty cross-canter for a few lazy strides or partway into turns, and more than one successful Olympic jumping round or barrel racing run has included quite a few cross-canter strides. Still, while the occasional cross-canter stride may not be a cause for panic, it is nothing to be sought out. Habitual cross-cantering for long stretches is not something I have seen sound, supple horses do much. If a horse cross-canters more under saddle than they do at liberty, something is wrong with the work under saddle. If they cross-canter more when changing from one lead to the other, that also points to some asymmetry in horse or rider.

I get a charge out of this, too:

I love it when people say they are going to teach their young horses to change leads. The horse has been changing leads since it was three days old, while no human in the history of the species has ever cantered, much less changed leads. We have something to teach a horse about flying changes? Horse do these on a regular basis out in the field, but for some reason it can take years to "teach" this movement to the horse in the ring. Maybe we could let our horses teach us how they do that, instead?

THE GALLOP

The gallop is a four-beat gait with one prolonged phase of suspension, as follows:

1. Outside hind
2. Inside hind
3. Outside fore
4. Inside fore
5. Phase of suspension

The gallop is similar to the canter, except each foot lands and pushes off individually. At the gallop, the outside hind lands followed by the inside hind, as in the canter, but the inside hind is well along into its power stroke before the outside fore touches down. Its phases are different than the canter, too:

1. Outside hind (first beat, three legs in flight)
2. Outside hind and inside hind (inside hind touches down as second beat, both forelegs in flight)
3. Inside hind (outside hind has lifted, both forelegs still in flight)
4. Inside hind and outside fore (outside fore touches down as third beat)
5. Outside fore (both hind legs and inside fore in flight)
6. Outside fore and inside fore (inside fore touches down as fourth beat)
7. Inside fore (both hind legs and outside fore in flight)
8. Phase of suspension (all legs in flight)

A quick study of any issue of *The Blood Horse* will show that there is some variation in how the third and fourth phases of the gallop operate, possibly due to whether the horse is accelerating or tiring. But a galloping horse often has only one leg on the ground, and doesn't have three feet on the ground at any time. The phase of suspension is more prolonged than in the canter. The horse gains much more than one body length per gallop stride. The gallop is the most inherently energetic gait, and, with its long suspension and fewer points of support on the ground at one time, the most prone to imbalance.

This is a perfectly natural and enjoyable gait for horses, but less welcomed by some riders. Perhaps because it does take longer to slow down from a gallop, riders may feel that they have less control, so they never let their horses open up. Galloping is great fun with a fit horse that knows its job, on safe footing.

A smart gallop around a field with good footing is the quickest way to rouse a lazy horse, much better than endlessly circling an arena thumping it with leg and spur to try to get it interested. On the other hand, a horse that is already on the nervy side, or has become unaccustomed to work where there is room for a gallop, might not be able to handle the extra adrenaline. It is better to work up to longer gallops with slower work in small doses. But if you have enough room with good footing, are 110 percent sure you can handle it, and your horse is fit enough, a long gallop might remove the excess excitement factor.

Galloping requires a great deal of spinal flexibility from the horse, so developing the gallop can help all the paces by activating the spine and topline, the ultimate source of all movement. The gallop will also trim up a sagging belly, and with well-planned work, improve heart and lung capacity. However, it is easy to overburden soft tendons and ligaments and lung capacity before you even approach serious cardiovascular training levels. Be sure your galloping work comes after the horse's legs and lungs are fit enough to take it, so your horse's wheels don't start falling off before you have gotten any cardiovascular benefit from it.

An efficiently galloping or cantering horse lets the gait's rocking action assist their breathing. Their guts slosh back and forth in their barrel with the rocking action of these gaits and act rather like bellows on their diaphragm and lungs. A horse that breathes out of rhythm with its canter or gallop stride will have very little staying power, but many horses that do use the rhythm of the stride will make a pleasantly soft nostril flutter as they exhale with every stride. A horse whose respiratory apparatus is constricted or has been damaged will make whistling or even "roaring" sounds, which are altogether different.

It is also true that if you gallop every time you come to a certain place or even a certain kind of place, like every open field, your horse will quickly start to anticipate your pattern. Be very sure that is what you will really always want to happen!

THE REINBACK

Backing up is not something horses like to do for many strides, but they can all do it and some of them get very good at it. Backing up is rather like a trot in reverse, with no phase of suspension:

1. Outside hind and inside fore together (other diagonal pair in flight)
2. Inside hind and outside fore together (other diagonal pair in flight)

The phases of reinback are the same as its footfall.

The diagonal pairs should move together in a distinct two-beat with clearly lifting feet, rather than stiff legs dragging each foot back through the dirt one at a time. The reinback's lack of suspension and energy level hold the same seeds of resistance as for the walk, with the additional factor that horses cannot see if they are backing into something directly behind them. The reinback is also prone to becoming crooked, with the horse traveling a curve rather than a straight line. This comes from one hind leg not being quite as good at pushing forward under the horse's belly to draw the horse's body backward. An active, rhythmic, and straight reinback is an excellent indicator of the horse's symmetrical development, trust, dexterity, and suppleness.

Prolonged reinbacks are hard on a horse's hocks and back, so they should be developed gradually. However, a prompt and straight reinback for at least a few steps is a requirement for any good saddle horse and especially for trail horses and hunters. It can be the only way out of trouble at times.

Reinbacks are often used to "get a horse back on its hindquarters," which really means getting the hind leg(s) to work far forward under the horse's belly. A horse with a hind leg well forward under its belly is in a good position to lift and spin its forehand around to that side, so a reinback is sometimes used to set a horse up for quick turns called rollbacks or spins.

Reining back is also sometimes used as a punishment, although I don't see the sense in using something we do want the horse to do as a punishment. If a reinback does work as a punishment, I suspect that is because it is done roughly rather than correctly. Why would I want to teach the horse to reinback wrongly or that reining back is uncomfortable? Like any exercise that calls for frequent transitions, a series of halts and reinbacks may make a horse more attentive, but not necessarily any better than some other transition combinations.

A horse cannot go directly into a reinback from any forward gait. There has to be at least a momentary halt/pause to shift gears. However, with a powerful enough push from the hind leg(s), a horse can go directly from a reinback into the forward gaits. Bonus questions: how similar are the phases of the reinback to the various phases of each of the forward gaits? What would be a good moment for a reinback/canter transition on the inside lead?

Be careful that your horse always moves forward promptly out of a reinback, lest it develop backing up as an evasion. The common wisdom is that horses that evade by backing up are one bad step away from becoming rearers. At the very least, these horses do not respect leg aids. The horse may have good reason for that, but it is a fundamental problem to be dealt with by very, very experienced riders. It may be that the horse is simply afraid of the rider's hands. There are also quite a few different recommended ways to signal a horse to back up; maybe the rider inadvertently hit a "reinback button" and the horse is doing exactly what it was trained to do. Those are all different than a horse who uses backing up as an evasion. It is not uncommon to see inexperienced riders pull on the reins to stop a horse when it backs up. Things can get unnerving if the horse backs up even faster as a result. The way to get a horse to stop backing up is to get the horse moving forward again, not to pull on the reins.

WHY DO WE NEED TO LEARN ALL THIS?

With a clear understanding of what horses are doing at each of the basic gaits, we can use dance-like communication with the horse to change from one to the other (transitions between gaits) or to change the length and height of the strides within each gait (transitions within the gait or tempo changes), and any of the other movements various sports call for.

When you are dancing with a partner and you want your partner to take a bigger step, do you:

A) Poke your partner in the ribs, or

B) Say, "Take a bigger step now, please," or

C) Use a signal you agree on beforehand that means "bigger step," or

D) Take a bigger step yourself?

Answer A) would no doubt work but will not make you a popular dance partner if that's your typical way of dancing. Answer B) could work, too, especially when you are first learning a dance, but it is rather slow and won't work at all if the person doesn't know what you mean by some words or can't hear you. Answer C) can work if you have worked out every signal you will ever need for every dance you will ever do, are sure you both understand and use the same set of signals, and you never inadvertently use the foxtrot signal when you meant to use the waltz signal. Answer D) will always work for every step of every dance if your partner has agreed simply to dance with you and you time your moves well with your partner's steps.

What does this mean in riding terms?

We can physically compel a horse to do some things, and that may be necessary at times for the horse's or our own safety. But going about things like that as a general rule makes most horses grumpy and insensitive. We can teach the horse what we mean by various words or sounds like clucking, and then just tell the horse what we want it to do. This is often used very successfully with young horses, although I eventually realized that is asking an awful lot from an animal that is not naturally primarily a verbal communicator. When you think about it, it is remarkable how easily they pick up on spoken language and that they go along with it so readily. This can be useful until we get into competitions where speaking is not allowed or encounter situations we don't have a word for. It is always much slower and limited than communication by physical contact.

We can certainly train a horse that we want it to do certain things when we touch it certain ways: a leg pressure here means this, rein pressure there means that, and so on. This works very well to the extent we spend virtually all of our training time working these signals out and keeping them in operation and have a signal for everything we will ever want a horse to do under every circumstance it may encounter. For example, let's say we teach a horse to stand like a rock when it hears or sees chain saws. That's great when you and your horse are out supervising the logging crew. It may not work the way you intended when your horse hears a chain saw when you are in the middle of a gallop circle in a reining pattern. Your horse may get confused when you object to stopping at that moment, and you may get confused later when your horse no longer stands when it encounters chain saws. It won't work out well at all if you ever get chased by a chain saw murderer.

Another problem with a signal-based system is that people do not necessarily agree on the signals to be used even for standard things. One rider might raise the reins to get a stop, another might pull them back, and another might lay them on the horse's neck. Over the years, I have been taught at least six different ways to get a horse to canter, including prodding the horse's outside elbow with my toe or lifting my seat out of the saddle. They all worked on the horses that were taught that signal. Horses don't care what signals we use. However elaborate our justification for our favorite set of signals, horses will learn what we teach them. But what happens when a rider doesn't know the signals the horse was taught, or vice versa? The rider might get surprised, even dangerously so, when a horse slams to a stop if the rider lowers their hands onto the horse's neck before a jump. So, C) works very well to a point, but does have limitations in the long run.

Answer D), however, has every advantage in terms of universal application and easy application. It requires only that the rider understand what they are asking the horse to do, and how to make it easy for the horse to change what they are doing at the moment to what we want to happen next. This does put the responsibility for good communication on the rider. Since we are supposed to be smarter than horses, I think that is the right thing to do.

CHAPTER 5

Summing Up and Drawing Conclusions So Far

Think first of the end.
—Leonardo da Vinci

"The seat comprises two major parts; 50 percent is formed by the rider, the other
50 percent is made up by the horse. However, both of these equal portions are
entirely the responsibility of the rider."
—Erik Herbermann

We can call this way of sitting a horse and using its motion to our advantage a seamless seat. A seamless seat has three significant advantages: comfort, good diagnostics, and clarity of communication.

COMFORT FOR HORSE AND RIDER

From the horse's viewpoint, problems rarely come from carrying weight as such. The rider's imbalance, immobility, or bad timing are generally much more of a problem. Would you rather carry a ton of lead or ton of feathers?

A horse that feels the rider as very quiet in relation to its movement need not defend itself physically or mentally against the rider's seat's bips and pops and friction. At a minimum, it doesn't make sense for the rider to be part of the horse's problem, especially right when the horse is trying to do what we want it to do.

A seamless seat is also comfortable for the rider. Obviously, not having any bips, pops, flaps, friction, or rubs is nicer than getting jostled and tossed and beat up by the horse's motion. Comfort makes for longer rides. That means more fun without using yourself and your horse up. That's a good thing.

RELIABLE DIAGNOSTICS

We need to know what the horse is doing before we can decide if we want to change it. It may seem straightforward enough to at least know what gait a horse is doing, but even that isn't always so clear. We often see beginners posting for quite a few strides after the horse falls back into a walk, for example. A more experienced rider might be quite surprised to find out she was on the wrong (or right!) lead at the canter, or failed to judge whether her horse's stride would get them over a trail obstacle or jump easily.

Perhaps even more riders are surprised when the horse seems to "suddenly" spook or run out at a fence. It is far more common for a horse to lead up to these events stride by stride, almost as if it is asking permission to screw up, or, perhaps more likely, asking for better guidance. The horse may also be showing as clearly as it can that it does not think things will work out well if it does obey the rider. A rider with a more receptive seat would be aware something was up earlier in the game, and he could take care of small problems instead of waiting for them to get worse and harder to deal with.

Good diagnostics also help us discover our horse's physical strong and weak points. Then we can build workouts that develop the weaker parts sensibly. Good diagnostics mean we can give the horse more sensible gymnastic tasks and be better gym teachers.

Until we have gotten that job done, at least we won't get in trouble by calling on an ability the horse does not have to give us. If we haven't gotten that gymnastisizing job done sufficiently for the task at hand at the moment, at least we know that the horse is going to go about things differently on the left hand than the right. That might be a good thing to know when you have a trail with lots of trees and hills and turns in front of you. It can save your knees quite a few bruises.

Subtle changes in your horse's strides and steps may not be obvious until your diagnostic skills are refined, but that doesn't mean the information isn't there. It means it is worthwhile to become more aware of increasingly subtle information from horses. Once you start looking for these things, it isn't all that difficult to figure out what the horse's physical status is, down to what muscle group might need some suppling work. This often happens intuitively anyway. Even rather inexperienced riders sense that some things are easier for the horse than others. From that beginning, it is quite easy to develop and refine a sense of what gymnastic help the horse needs.

If a seamless seat keeps you aware of developing irregularities, workouts can be much better tuned to the horse's needs. That leads to better-trained, more accurately controlled, and sounder horses. When my horse is well gymnasticized, I might not have to have the massage therapist out every other week and buy every new saddle pad that promises to relieve back pain. Solid diagnostics are good for your performance and for your pocketbook.

CLEARER COMMUNICATION WITH THE HORSE

If there are no bips, pops, or rubs between the horse and the rider, the horse experiences the rider as very quiet. It would be like someone just laying their hand on your back or shoulder as you walk along, versus someone rubbing or tapping or clutching on you. A rider that is quiet in relation to the horse's movement is like the difference between a pleasant hum versus random static from a radio. It's harder to sort out the music over a lot of static.

If the horse experiences the rider as generally very quiet in relation to its movement, the messages we do send are more likely to be understood as messages. The horse can become desensitized to our messages without our realizing a messy seat taught our horse to ignore us. If the horse gets accustomed to a certain amount of bipping and popping and rubbing, it can't be easy to sort out which the rider intended as messages and which are just the rider bumping as usual. The messages we do send would have to be harder than the usual bipping and popping and rubbing the horse has successfully ignored. So, a seamless interface with the horse means our messages can be more clearly understood by the horse as messages, and our horse would be more responsive to lighter aids.

Just like a good conversationalist and a good teacher have excellent listening skills, probably the most important part of riding is to develop a receptive, quiet seat. The main challenge some riders have finding a seamless interface with their horse is that they are not accustomed to riding being easy, just like listening takes fewer muscles than does speaking.

Luckily, we have all the physical and learning skills we need to improve in every stride. We may be amazed how quickly vicious cycles that seem unbreakable can turn into permanent virtuous cycles. With the learning and physical discovery tools we now have at hand, we can easily find and make the change that makes a difference.

How Can We Use All of This?

How the horse moves the rider is 100 percent diagnostic of what the horse is doing. Riders who become the most acutely aware of their horse's motion will be best able to understand and lead the conversation the way they want it to go. Knowing what the horse is doing with its feet when we ask it to do something can make our communication with the horse much easier for it to understand. We can also better measure the gymnastic demands we are making on the horse. The more sensitive we are to changes in the horse's motion and any patterns to these changes, the better gym teachers and religion teachers we can be.

Riders who can identify and take care of small changes in what the horse is doing can prevent small problems from accumulating into big problems. Irregularities and asymmetries need not be repeated until they become a confirmed bad habit. If you didn't know there was a change in the horse's motion at all, you could end up inadvertently promoting physical patterns you won't want and discouraging changes you will want. More important, if you can identify small changes that are more like what you do want to happen, you can promote those, too. Riders who are sensitive to their interface with the horse have the most accurate communication with the horse. It's the changes we did not know we made that cause confusion.

Riders who are sensitive to their interface with the horse have a personal and immediate way to evaluate their seat. They can use the horse's motion to help make any seat corrections or experiments they want to try. What you think is a mistake may well turn out not be one at all. Short of obviously dangerous things, try some new things before you decide they are mistakes and always would be mistakes under any circumstances. Like a weed is just a plant in the wrong place, what isn't working in one situation may be just the ticket in another.

Exaggerating something is also a great way to learn more about it. When you know what too much is, you know more about what is enough. You may find that you were on the right track; the question then is not what to do, but how much to do.

Riders with the most sensitive interface with their horse can learn a lot about the horse by how the horse moves them. That could explain a lot of their behavior, their ability to respond to our aids, and their physical development.

Horses start out quite sensitive to the rider when they are first ridden. Although they may find it awkward, especially if they are not well gymnasticized for their job beforehand, they are certainly very aware of how we feel to them as riders. Similarly, you are most aware of how a backpack sits when you first put it on, and probably least agile carrying it unless you are already in good shape for that job.

Whether a horse's first few rides encourages it to ignore or heed the sensations the rider causes depends on how we hold up our end of the conversation. Horses will learn to heed whatever level of sensitivity we teach them that turns out well for them, whether we mean to teach them that or not.

Gymnastic Development as a Priority

Making gymnastic development a priority is the way I like to deal with horses from a personal philosophy, but there is all the reason in the world to use it for competitive and financial reasons, too. Accessing the horse's full talents and keeping it sound are some very direct results of going about things with the horse's gymnastic development as your first priority. As Alois Podhajsky, a fellow who knew all about developing horses' full athletic potential even beyond Olympic demands and keeping them in world-class trim well into their twenties, says, good athletic development makes a horse more beautiful. That's money in the bank.

This still counts if you are not a professional or not planning on going to the Olympics. The most beautiful horse in the world is still at risk if it can't perform some job. A sound and capable horse of any quality is always going to be able to at least find a good home, should that ever become an issue. Far better to have a horse that is easily marketable at any moment, even if you do not foresee the need. Things happen and people change. No sense in making what to do with our horse any harder a part of larger problems life may hand us than it needs to be.

It is rather easy to get stuck on favorite ground exercises, school figures, or pleasant riding trails without considering the gymnastic demands our work puts on the horse. That can lead to believing we have more control over the horse than we really have, or that our horse is more skilled and physically well developed than it really is. We may not realize asymmetry and unevenness are gradually causing chronic lameness in our horses and bad backs or knees in ourselves.

Getting stuck on certain rituals, especially anything involving getting the horse to put its head in any particular place, or reaching certain spots in an arena, often leads us to believe we have more understanding than is true.

If we focus on *what* the horse is doing (walk, trot, canter, figure-eights, voltes, sliding stops, etc.) more than how the horse is going about things (gymnastically beneficially), we can be setting ourselves and our horses up for physical and mental obstacles.

Riding to explore and expand the conditions under which the horse can maintain a gymnastically beneficial way of going about its job is altogether different than doing many jobs gymnastically poorly, even though the patterns ridden may be the same. When gymnastic development comes first, accuracy and obedience and therefore performance and safety will improve as the horse becomes more physically able to comply with our aids. We can then use their talents to the fullest. As horses have more reason to believe we do see things from their point of view, they tend to get more communicative. We may not always agree with them, but at least we can take their viewpoint into account.

The way we sit on horses very much determines what the horse experiences when it's under saddle and the gymnastic effort it has to make to do the job we asked for. Since horses learn mostly from their physical experience, our seat and therefore our aids can make a big difference in how easily the horse can learn what we meant to teach them. Luckily, the solution is remarkably simple. If our priority becomes doing everything with the minimum possible effort for the maximum possible outcome, if we attend to how we are doing things (elegantly) instead of just *what* we are doing (canter at a certain spot, for example, even if awkwardly), the sky is suddenly the limit. That might take some search image revisions, which in turn requires mental clarity and physical sensitivity.

Luckily, we are actually already very good at sending and receiving physical messages and measuring the gymnastic demands of any activity, so applying those skills to riding shouldn't be difficult at all.

SUMMARY

A good seat is not a position. It is a way of using the horse's movement to our advantage to gain security, accurate feedback, and clear communication. Form is not an end in itself; it's an arrangement from which we can best receive information, clearly evaluate events, and participate in a two-way body language conversation. A good seat is the tool we use to find out how to be secure and effective riders. It is the portal through which we learn about horses under saddle.

We now know quite a bit about how to tell what the horse is doing, and we know quite a bit about how to see to it the horses experience us as riders the way we intend them to. Now we can start considering how to put this all together to make it easy for the horse to understand and do what we want to do.

How can it be that the answer to fluid, effortless riding has been right at our fingertips, but we learned the hard way, instead? There are quite a few perfectly normal reasons, some of which we will look at in the next chapter.

We will see next how to use these ideas to communicate most clearly with our horses, so we can most easily teach them whatever we want them to learn. We will take a look at some learning tactics first, and then at the tools we have to communicate with the horse: the aids. Then we can put it all together to see how to get where we want to go in whatever sport we choose.

CHAPTER 6

Learning about Anything, Including Riding

I know but one freedom, and that is freedom of the mind.
—Antoine de Saint-Exupery

The great enemy of truth is often not the lie—deliberate, contrived, and dishonest—
but the myth—persistent, persuasive, and unrealistic.
—John F. Kennedy

As we experiment with our best physical arrangement on the horse, we are bound to wonder how we learned the habits we have learned. Here are some interesting viewpoints about how we may not be learning as efficiently as we could.

WHAT WE SEE VERSUS WHAT IS REALLY GOING ON

Henry Wynmalen says the best horseman is the most observant horseman. Indeed, he says the measure of a trainer's talent is the ability to spot at once the slightest indication of the horse's thoughts coming round in the desired direction—close and accurate observation, indeed!

Obviously, we can only respond to what we perceive, but just because I don't see a hundred-dollar bill lying on the sidewalk doesn't mean it isn't there. Oversight or misperception doesn't change its value. Seeing things for what they are can be very worthwhile, although we often see only what we expect to see.

We may be wired by Nature to react before we think too much, but I believe people hang on to misperceptions in a worthy effort to retain the knowledge gained so far. This may be especially true if we believe we have reached a satisfactory level of skill and don't need to progress any further as riders. However, this limits us to our previous knowledge, which could be dangerous and harder on our horses and ourselves than need be. Endlessly repeating what we have already done is also ultimately boring. Merely changing the trails we ride or the shows we attend eventually gets old, whereas gaining insight into what goes into the simplest trail ride or show round can be endlessly fascinating.

We often have much more ability than we allow ourselves to show or exercise, and I believe we all know this at heart. Our satisfaction has to do with the kind of continual improvement that makes the occasional flashes of really good riding we all experience now and again so frequent they become our normal way of riding.

Let's take a look at some of the ways we overlook what is there to be seen, and therefore limit ourselves unnecessarily. One of many schools of thought about how people think and learn is called Neuro-linguistic Programming (NLP). Here are some real and some imagined scenarios that demonstrate some useful NLP ideas.

NLP-isms

GENERALIZATION, DISTORTION, AND DELETION

The way things do go sometimes, case 1:

You see a small, fat, gray horse spooking for no apparent reason. You may easily "remember" the horse as an Arab, if you think Arabs are commonly gray, small, fat, and spooky. Actually, the spooky horse could be a young Connemara at its first show and it just heard loudspeakers squeal for the first time. You may not notice the perfectly calm Arab standing not ten feet away from the bug-eyed Connemara.

The way things could go sometimes:

When you see a spooky horse, you take a moment to consider that it might have a good reason for spooking, regardless of its breed. You then realize you hadn't noticed the loudspeaker squealing as quickly as the young horse did. You may also note that the horse was too stocky to be an Arab. You've learned new information, rather than confirming a stereotype.

The way things do go sometimes, case 2:

You are in quite a good mood and pleased with how nicely your horse is doing on the trails. As you clean her up, you notice that the sweat mark under the saddle is lopsided again. Your saddle pad must still be slipping to the side. That might also explain why she's a little ouchy along her back. Maybe it's time to get a new saddle pad. What your instructor had said about sitting squarely on your horse doesn't enter your mind.

The way things could go sometimes:

You start looking for at least three more reasons the saddle mark could be crooked and your horse's back is tender, and how you can figure out what the problem really is. You save yourself some money on a saddle pad that wouldn't fix the problem anyway and develop a plan to test your new theories.

The way things do go sometimes, case 3:

You see one of the winning show horses looking sort of dozy and the groom slipping something into her pocket with a worried glance at you as you walk by the stall. She pocketed a syringe! Like they didn't already have enough of an advantage, as much money as they must have!

The way things could go sometimes:

You look again and notice a fellow with a stethoscope and a stainless steel bucket getting out of a pickup and heading for the colicky champion. You realize the groom had been examining the horse's eyes and gums with one of those mini-flashlights. You think one of those little flashlights could be useful in your show tack trunk, too, and it would also make a neat gift for a friend of yours. You make your life and your friend's life better and admit that not all champions are created just from money, or all millionaire riders would be champions.

MODELING SUCCESS LEADS TO EXCELLENCE

The way things do go sometimes:

This is your first time in the novice reining class. No one expects much more of you than to remember the pattern. But you know in your heart that one day you could be as good as Doug Mulholland. A pattern like this would be so easy for him, he'd knock it out just for a warm-up while he whistled "Amazing Grace." He'd do it like this, and this, and this.

The way things could go sometimes:

Next thing you know, you're looking at your first blue ribbon. You decide to pretend you are Doug Mulholland in your training sessions, too.

CONTRASTIVE ANALYSIS

The way things do go sometimes, case 1:

As you review your lesson notes, you think about the jumps that were particularly pleasant and start comparing those with the rest of the jumps and with other riding experiences. You realize that every time there was kind of a bump as you landed, you heard a hoof thunk on the jump pole. The jumps that felt very smooth didn't come with those same thunking sounds. Hmmmm . . .

The way things could go sometimes:

You imagine each jump in great detail: what it felt like, what it looked like, what it sounded like before, during, and after the jump. You decide to watch your lesson buddies to see what is going on when the horses hit the rails and to watch a few videos of the Olympic jumpers to see what seems to lead to horses hitting the jump poles. You realize there are many ways to learn about riding outside the arena, too.

HAVING A CHOICE IS BETTER
THAN NOT HAVING A CHOICE

The way things do go sometimes:

Your riding would be so different if only you had more time for it. Or more money, so you could hire a cook and a nanny.

The way things could go sometimes:

You make a list of all the ways you could arrange your time better. You could trade babysitting with your neighbors. You could get together with some of your riding buddies and have a neighborhood teenager watch the kids at the barn while you all ride, maybe even arrange for pony rides. You could cook a roast beef and pork roast on Fridays, prepare two meals at the same time, and freeze one to reheat when you got back from riding. You could make Saturday the official grill night, since your husband likes to do that. You start making phone calls about arranging for babysitters at the barn and call the barn manager to see if that might work. Your friends get more riding time, your barn manager is glad to see more action at the barn, and a local teen makes some pocket money.

PEOPLE (AND HORSES) ARE
MORE THAN THEIR BEHAVIOR

The way things do go sometimes:

Miss Muffet was a little gray who, like most Davenport Arabians, seemed to have been born trained and devoted to their person's happiness. Since Muffet was rock solid, I let a rather timid lady at the barn ride her at times.

I was surprised to hear one evening that Muffet had been really bad that day. It had all started when Muffet was apparently startled by sunlight glinting off a shovel lying in a sawdust pile in the corner of the arena as usual. Within minutes, Muffet was leaping away from corner, reaching the middle of the arena in two bounds, which is rather a trick for a 14-hand animal.

"It's just not like her. It was like she was seeing a ghost," the rider declared.

"What did she do once she got to the middle of the arena?" I asked. "Did she keeping looking at the corner and snorting and such?"

"No. She just stood there like nothing had happened. So I'd start around the arena again, and she'd be just fine until we got to that corner again. She'd trot along just fine until a couple strides before the shovel, and then she'd suddenly just leap away."

"So she wasn't afraid of going toward the corner?"

"Well, she must be, or why would she jump away from it?"

"Did you fall off?"

"No," the lady declared proudly. Knowing that she was not the most secure of riders, I figured the leaps were probably not quite as sudden and wild as described, but still a cause for concern.

"What did you do, the first time she startled at the shovel?"

"Well, I tried to reassure her, of course. I pet her a lot. Really, I did."

"Uh huh. And so she repeated the same thing the next time, and you pet her even more?"

"Sure! When she stopped in the middle, I even gave her carrots. Nothing seemed to work! It was getting worse and worse, so after about four more times, I got off."

"Why in the world would you pet a horse and give it carrots for doing something you don't want it to do?"

"What? What am I supposed to do? Beat her? It isn't right to beat a horse, especially when it's scared. I simply won't do it."

"Of course not, except she wasn't scared anyway. She was doing exactly what you were rewarding her for doing. Just tell her to go about her business, if that's what you want her to do."

"Well, I think scared horses should be reassured. Don't you?"

"Sure. When did I say anything else?"

The way things could go sometimes:

You start training Muffet to bow when you are getting ready to mount, since she knows everything else already and it only takes about five minutes to teach her anything.

EVERY BEHAVIOR HAS A POSITIVE INTENT

The way things do go sometimes:

People just don't appreciate how considerate and respectful you really are. You saw Fred was having a hard time loading his horse, but you are quite sure he is a good enough horseman to take care of the situation and would rather work it out with his horse by himself anyway. You just wanted to get your car out of his way, and then he got mad at you for driving off without even offering to help when he was in a rush.

A few days later, your instructor gave you a hard time because you got the wrong lead every darn time. You wish he would explain more about how the outside leg works, but you missed a lot of what he was saying because your horse was shifting his hindquarters around a lot right then. Plus, you didn't want to hold the whole class up. You wanted to ask some questions after the ride, except you thought your instructor was in a bad mood today.

Meanwhile, your instructor is wishing people would simply say so when they didn't catch something the first time. No one says a word when he asks for questions. Are they too proud to admit they didn't catch it? It's not like it won't be obvious whether they understood or not, once they start trying the exercise. He wonders if he'll ever get a really serious group of students to work with.

The way things could go sometimes:

You make an effort to check if people are looking for your input more often. You find out they really do want to know what you are up to, you solidify some friendships, and make the lessons more lively, to boot.

EVERYONE HAS ALL THE RESOURCES THEY NEED TO ACHIEVE THEIR DESIRED OUTCOMES

The way things do go sometimes:

The total training equipment used by one very successful FEI level jumper rider is said to consist of two jump standards and a pole. One of the most successful show jumpers in history started out as a cart horse. More than one cheap racehorse has made it to the Breeder's Cup and beaten horses that cost half a million dollars as yearlings.

The way things could go sometimes:

You decide you don't have to shop for the most fashionable breastplate this year after all, which saves some time and money for a few more lessons before the show.

YOU CANNOT NOT COMMUNICATE

The way things do go sometimes:

Your teacher said your lesson went well enough, but something in her voice and, well, just the way she said it, told you she was disappointed.

After you put the horse away and you are signing up for your next lesson, it somehow seems like next week is going to be really busy. You decide to call later, after you take a closer look at your calendar.

You instructor mentally makes a note that she will probably have a little free time next week during your usual lesson slot.

The way things could go sometimes:

You ask your instructor if there was anything more specific she can tell you about your ride. She'd noticed he seemed to be holding back some, but hadn't quite figured out why. You end up in an interesting discussion about some new shoeing techniques that might help your horse move better. You ask a friend to video your next lesson for your farrier to see what your instructor noticed. You realize your instructor has a vantage point, concerns, and resources you hadn't considered fully before.

IF SOMETHING ISN'T WORKING, DO SOMETHING DIFFERENT

The way things do go sometimes:

God knows you've been patient with that beast. You've wiped out the carrot supply at the local grocer's for that dumb, ungrateful, lazy, deceitful nag. It's the same every time. You go out to the field with a bag of carrots and a halter, and you return with the halter, no carrots, and no horse.

And a voice seems to speak to you, saying:

"If you always do what you've always done, you'll always get what you always got."

Next time, by golly, you swear you are either coming back with the horse or the carrots.

The way things could go sometimes:

You realize that you have been trying to bribe your horse into being caught rather than rewarding him when he agrees to be caught. Treats used to work back when he was so nervous about everything, but that stopped working some time ago. Now, you can try some other plans. You could ask the barn manager not to turn him out. Or leave a halter on him. Or just work on catching him every day for the next two weeks or so. Or you could learn to throw a lariat. You also realize you horse has gained more confidence than you thought and think you could try pushing his training just a little bit further now.

THERE IS NO FAILURE, ONLY FEEDBACK

The way things do go sometimes:

A fellow had a nice horse with which he wanted to do cavalry reenactments. The horse was terrific about everything except the pistols. So, the rider decided to get him used to pistols with some calm, controlled round pen work.

The guy took his pistol out of the holster and the horse started dancing around nervously as soon as he saw it. The guy put the pistol back, calmed the horse down, and tried again. With each go-round, the horse would get more nervous more quickly, until the horse was dancing around in panic as soon as he saw the guy's hand approaching the holster.

The way things could go sometimes:

The guy kept the pistol well out in the open and let the horse dance around until the horse had four feet on the ground for a split second, as was bound to happen eventually, probably as the horse hesitated for a moment while he was changing directions. The guy put the pistol back in the holster

ASAP every time the horse had all four feet on the ground even for an instant. Within about 10 minutes, the horse began to figure out that putting his feet on the ground would get the fellow to put the pistol away. Within about 20 minutes, the horse was standing like a rock with the pistol in clear view. The fellow learned that he had misunderstood his horse's approach to teaching his person what to do when he was scared, and the horse learned his person was getting smarter all the time.

THE MEANING OF ANY COMMUNICATION
IS THE RESPONSE IT GETS

The way things do go sometimes:

A student of mine hadn't really caught on to leg yielding, but one evening when she was working on trot transitions, she did a lovely leg yield from the quarterline to the track. It was like she'd been doing it all her life, just as smooth and forward and rhythmic as you could possibly want. "That was terrific!" I said. "Very nice, indeed! Well ridden!"

"What are you talking about?!" she replied. "I can't get the darn horse to trot!"

"Ah, that. Well, yeah, you didn't get a trot, but you sure did get a beautiful leg yield."

"But it was wrong!"

"It wasn't what you expected, but it wasn't wrong at all. It was as correct a leg yield as I have ever seen. According to your horse, it seems what you think is a trot aid is a perfect leg yield aid. Now, how could that be?"

That might have been that rider's first real clue how much different her left leg aids were than her right leg aids.

The way things could go sometimes:

The next time your horse leg yields instead of trotting, you take it as a lesson in leg yielding and review all of the sensations and communications that produced the leg yield. You might also contrast that with some recent trot transitions.

ANYTHING SOMEONE ELSE CAN DO CAN BE LEARNED

The way things do go sometimes:

Before Caprilli developed what has become the modern jumping technique, four feet was considered a spectacularly high jump. His new ideas were widely criticized, especially on the basis of safety. However, when he and his students started being virtually unbeatable in the jumping ring, more people started to adopt his methods. Today, what would once have been considered wonderful form over a fence ("hailing a cab") would be considered a major flaw even for a beginner over fences.

The way things could go sometimes:

Instead of assuming that second-level dressage is too advanced for you and all that trotting would not be good for a reining horse anyway, you decide that you should learn more about what dressage and reining might have in common. A few months later, your reining scores have jumped skyward and you have taken a few dressage ribbons, too.

STAGES OF LEARNING

NLP divides learning into four stages.

1. Unconscious incompetence—As a novice, or anytime we try something new, we may well feel things are going along quite well, happily unaware of how much more there is to learn about a new endeavor and how far from expert we are. As we learn more about what is involved, we may decide not to pursue the activity further, or we may move to the next stage.

2. Conscious incompetence—With a bit more experience, and as we begin to assimilate standards of good performance, we realize we weren't doing as well as we thought we were. This can be tough on one's ego. If we decide to continue, this is often the stage at which we

begin to plan for our desired future level of competence and start identifying the particular challenges that may remain with us for some time. As we start overcoming those challenges, we may move on to the next stage.

3. Conscious competence—With effort and under controlled circumstances, we can pull off increasingly better performances. We have gained a good deal of background and technical knowledge and are better able to identify what makes top performers unique, although how top level performance can be achieved personally may not be clear. We may question if it is realistic to try to achieve our previous goals. They may look more complicated than they did at first.

4. Unconscious competence—Our current highest level of skill stays intact even under previously unencountered situations. As the saying goes, our worst is better than our best used to be without significant rehearsal or preparation. A higher level of skill becomes routine. Preparatory work and competition performance are indistinguishable. A high level of unconscious competence is when, as one high level rider had been known to say, the Olympics are just another horse show.

We may move through these stages more than once in riding, as we attempt new aspects of riding, or new levels of performance in the same sport. For example, an accomplished student may encounter a certain kind of unconscious incompetence when first working with young horses. A successful amateur might view his previous accomplishments in a new light when he moves into open competition ranks.

This keeps riding fresh when we need a new challenge and heartening when we want to savor our accomplishments.

Aspirations, Motivations, and Assumptions

Are you satisfied with your riding? If so, or if you figure you can't do better, or don't need to do better even if you could, or you don't look forward to someone else telling you what to do to get better, it doesn't matter how many lessons you take. There would be no reason or pleasure in learning more.

However, people rarely do things for just one reason. If one of your goals in riding is to get out of the house, you've gotten one reward as soon as you've shut the door behind you. If one of your goals is to prove how tough and adventurous you are, bruises and sprains and near-misses will be signs of success to you. If one of your goals is to get in touch with your inner cowboy, you aren't likely to be satisfied training fine harness horses unless that could lead to driving a chuck wagon. If one of your goals is to prove you have lots of money, that's really easy to do with horses, and please give me a call!

NLP calls these latent motivators "secondary goals." Your riding will be satisfactory to you to the extent it agrees with all of your motivations, as well as your view of yourself and what you think riding "should" be like. Secondary goals may not be the stated goals and they may not be at all obvious or deliberate, but they can be very compelling. If you find you are not achieving your stated goals, check whether there is some secondary goal that conflicts with your stated goal.

Our basic, often unacknowledged, assumptions about ourselves and horses will also show up in how we go about things in general and with particular horses. If you believe in your heart that horses are inherently gentle and innocent, your way of going about things will work great with horses for whom that is true. If you feel a particular horse cooperates only because it figures it has to, you are going to handle it differently than someone who thinks it likes its work. If you believe horses are capable of an intelligent two-way conversation, you may find horses telling you more than you wanted to know.

It is very true that muscles do react when we just think about doing something, or imagine something happening. Horses respond to that level of muscle action. Clever Hans, the horse that appeared to be able to do math, proved that to scientists about 125 years ago. When presented with an arithmetic problem, Hans pawed until he reached the right number. Someone eventually realized Hans was responding to his owner's and even the crowd of spectators' unconsciously hopeful body language. It seems he was really pawing until he saw people relax when he got far enough. This had gone unobserved for years by hundreds of onlookers, including leading scientists of the day. Who ever said horses are stupid or insensitive?

Horses are probably more aware of our basic assumptions than we are. So would you be, if you were on the receiving end of the actions that follow from our basic assumptions about horses, riding, and ourselves. This can be an extremely powerful tool for good or bad. For example, simply not getting nervous yourself on a spooky horse makes for fewer spooks, and the spooks that do happen become no big deal to ride well. A rider's unintentionally defensive riding can easily tell a nervous horse the rider is concerned, too. This can put the horse on an even higher level of alert, so it spooks when it would otherwise be confident.

Other horses get upset when the rider acts concerned about something and they can't figure out what's wrong, since everything looks fine to them. It may well not occur to a horse that a rider is nervous about them, or a problem at work; they only know the person in charge is worried, so perhaps they should be, too. I also believe some horses just know they have a good chance to play a prank on the rider and do not realize their behavior can be dangerous for us.

As we learn more about our own and our horse's quirks, we may first suffer the disappointments of greater knowledge. Learning more about conformation also means learning many horses are not as pretty as we thought they were before we found out about ewe necks and poor hock angles, for example. Indeed, the more we learn, the fewer truly admirable horses seem to show up. When we are wiser, we will realize they are all beautiful, even the ugly ones, but we won't buy the one with horrible hocks as an Olympic prospect. We will also have an even finer appreciation for the truly great horses that we do see.

Similarly, discovering a physical or mental habit that was silently undermining our best riding can be discouraging at first. However, these discoveries also hold the promise of revealing talents we never suspected we had but were just waiting for their chance to shine.

So, let's see how our knowledge of our seat, the physical mechanics of human and horse movement, and our observation and learning skills can be combined into a clear and effective communication with our horses.

When I was in high school, I was riding a third-level dressage horse, by far the most highly trained horse I had ever ridden at the time. I was just supposed to canter a circle, but I couldn't get this mare to canter to save my life. The harder I tried, the worse it got. I was all over the saddle, the instructor was about to shoot me, and the mare would happily have handed him the gun. I had the sense to just stop. I'm ready to swear all I did was review in my mind the aids for the canter. Voilá! Off the mare went in a lovely canter. Halt-to-canter transitions are supposed to be a higher level movement than the canter circles I had been asked to do.

I can now cite all sorts of scientific studies that may explain why that worked so well, none of which could possibly be as instructive as the experience.

CHAPTER 7

There Are Only
So Many Ways to Sit

The most important teacher of the diligent rider's seat is the horse.
—Gustav Steinbrecht

Aiding is a perpetual, subtle form of rewarding.
—Charles de Kunffy

There is no secret so close as that between a rider and his horse.
—R. S. Surtees

We now know quite a bit about human body mechanics, the horse's gait mechanics, and about learning. These are the basic ingredients of riding in all horse sports, so now we can start considering how to mix these up into a recipe for success for you, on your horse, for your sport.

It may not be evident to a casual observer, but riders know our seat on our horse is a way of going about things rather than a particular posture. It lets us use the horse's motion to our advantage most easily for security and communication. Without security we will limit ourselves to what we already know. Without clear communications, we will limit ourselves in every way.

Our communication to the horse is often taken to mean signals or cues we have taught the horse. We often call our communication with the horse "aids" more out of convention than from taking the term in its literal sense: a way to assist the horse to do what we have in mind. However, talking about aiding our horse to canter, for example, with the idea of assisting the horse

128

to do so reveals an approach that is quite different than signaling our horse to canter.

We can teach a horse that certain ways we move or touch them mean we want the horse to canter, for example. That kind of signal-based communication system does work well up to a point. However, there is a universe beyond thinking about aids as signals, just as there is much more to any interesting conversation with friends than sending each other signals to sit, stand, smile, and walk.

Riding is basically a dance-like, two-sided conversation in body language about movement. We could speak the dialect of barrel racing, calf or fox chasing, jumping, marathon racing, and so on with our horses, but ultimately we are always speaking about moving feet. The only "signal" we need is for the horse to move the foot we ask for when we ask for it.

There are only four things we could possibly say to the horse about what it is doing with its feet, and, therefore, what it is doing with its whole body. We can:

1. Agree with what the horse is doing;
2. Ask for more of what it is doing;
3. Disagree with what it is doing; or,
4. Redirect what it is doing.

Everything we ask a horse to do comes down to how a horse's hind leg pushes off, swings forward/upward, and supports weight, and how that action travels along the horse's body. Each hind leg does its job in a certain sequence at each gait, as we have seen. If we can determine what the hind legs are doing and we have the horse lined up so that its movement travels along the spine the way we want, we can get a horse to perform anything a horse is capable of doing.

Horses have been doing most everything we will ever want them to do since they were about three days old. It's no mystery to the horse how to go from trot to canter, or swap leads, or piaffe or passage, or make a tight turn around an obstacle, or slide to a stop. So it is more accurate to say that riders can get a horse to do anything we understand well enough ourselves.

Riders may question whether a horse's response to aids can be relied on well enough to converse with specific feet. That is not necessarily what most riders seem to experience.

If horses can feel flies land on their coats, they are certainly physically sensitive enough to feel our physical communications. So if a horse is not responding as expected, my first question is: does the horse have any reason not to respond? If we make it easy for the horse to do what we have in mind, there is little reason to expect them to resist or ignore aids as a common thing.

My second question is: are you sure you asked for what you wanted, and didn't ask for anything else or contradict that in some way? The horse can be in a quandry if we constrict ourselves in some way when what we want from the horse is to move more freely, for example.

There are five tools we can use to tell the horse that we like what it is doing, we want more of what it is doing, we don't like what it is doing, or we would like it to do it in a different direction. These five pathways of communication, these five kinds of aids, will be presented here in the order they are to be used, based on the order of importance horses seem to place on the pathway of communication they receive.

The first item on the list happens before the other ones, because it is the horse's main source of information about their rider. Nothing comes before number one. It starts everything. It is numero uno, the first, the initiator, that-with-which-all-else-begins. That is to say, the first way we communicate with the horse is by how the horse experiences our platform, which we can also call our seat or weight aid.

There are four possible seat aids:

1. The passive seat, to agree with the horse's motion;
2. The active seat, to ask for more motion;
3. The limiting seat, to disagree with the horse's motion; and,
4. The unilateral seat, to redirect the horse's motion.

That covers everything our platform could possibly say to a horse about what it is doing.

The Passive Seat

Here's a good definition of the passive seat:

100 percent agreement of our platform with the horse's movement.

You can tell you have a good passive seat when there are no bips, pops, rubs, flops, rolls, or friction between your seat and the horse or saddle. There would be no change in the interface between the horse and the rider as the horse moves.

A passive seat says, "Nice, I like that. Carry on."

A passive seat is like nodding agreement when someone says something you like in a conversation. We even do that over the phone when our conversational partner can't possibly see us doing it. Surely we can do as much for our horses when we are sitting on them.

If you don't have a way to agree positively with what the horse is doing, how can your horse ever get the idea that anything it does is right? A pat and a kind word or a treat are good. However, making ourselves comfortable for the horse when it does anything that is even a little more like what we want is likely more important to the horse, and it's faster, too. Positive agreement with the horse's movement is surely the easiest, quickest, and most sensible reward we can give. It also keeps us riders releasing our own muscle tensions that can otherwise creep in among our holding patterns.

Getting too caught up in what we don't want the horse to do can overshadow what is going well. What you do want is one topic. What you don't want could be a list a hundred pages long. You'll spend so much time telling the horse no, you may never get around to discussing anything else.

There is something to like about every stride a horse takes. Even in the course of a major blow up, some foot somewhere is going to do something that is more like what we want, even if that isn't the horse's intention. If something is just a little more like what we want, then *tell the horse!* The best reward a horse can get is for the rider to become more comfortable, if only for that split second.

The better we get at catching the horse doing something right, or closer to right, the quicker the horse will catch on to the deal. When the horse finds it can do things that make the rider more comfortable to carry, it is likely to want to do those things.

So, the basic message about the passive seat is: at the very least, don't be part of the horse's problem.

The Active Seat

The second way we can use our seat is actively. We can define the active seat as:

even more agreement of your platform with the horse's motion.

It's one thing to listen carefully and nod in agreement with your conversational partner. It's another thing to add a smile, or applause, or any clear invitation for them to tell you more. That's an active seat.

An active seat says, "Yes! Give me more of what you are doing."

Now that we know quite a bit about the gaits, it is clear that your timing when you ask for something more says a lot about what your horse is likely to think you want more of and how promptly it can go along with the plan. It is also clear that each step might offer more than one way to convey what we want, which gives us greater flexibility in our communications than we can easily work into a signal-based system.

For example, let's say we want our horse to take longer strides. One way to get that is for the hind leg to swing more forward during the flight phase of the step, since the hind leg can't swing any farther forward once it has touched down. In an active seat, our platform can somewhat exaggerate the motion the horse is already offering us during the hind leg's flight phase.

You can also ask the horse for more during the push-off phase of a hind leg. Once a hind leg is in flight, it cannot add any more push to the stride. In an active seat, our platform can exaggerate the motion the horse is already offering us during the push-off phase. The horse can clearly understand and promptly respond to that request. Voila! One bigger flight phase or one bigger push-off accomplished with minimum effort. Repeat as and when needed.

The active seat is much like a dancer inviting a dance partner to take a bigger step by stepping bigger herself. This assumes the leading dancer knows when a bigger step is necessary and when her partner is in a good position to take the bigger step. If a longer step is required from your dancer partner's left foot, asking for that when the dancer partner's left foot is lifting and in the air will produce the desired response more quickly than when your dancer has just set that foot down. If you want a more powerful step, you would ask when your partner's foot is on the ground.

So, if your horse is lifting your platform upward and forward and that means the horse is already doing what you want more of at that gait, you can let the horse's motion start your platform on its way to allow the horse a little bit more room (and time) to lift upward and forward. You can let gravity slip your weight down the horse's sides and let the stirrups catch it.

It's perhaps subtle enough that it just feels like the horse magically volunteered a push that lifts your platform even more and improves your stirrup connection as your weight drops through your legs.

The active seat, like all aids, is a spectrum, not an on/off switch. We can be mildly active, or offer a very full range of motion for the horse to follow and still need some additional communication to get a big job done. We can use the horse's motion to be mildly active or more so, up to the point at which the horse begins to feel we are getting coercive or disconnected with our seat. There is only so far a rider can exaggerate a horse's motion without dropping a seatbone a bit more into the horse's back than the horse is comfortable with or standing a bit more away from the horse's back than the horse can follow.

As we saw earlier, the rider's freest range of motion comes most effectively from the hip joints, while the rider's vertebrae stay nicely stacked up. The angle between the entire upper body and the rider's thigh changes as the platform swings, rather than the rider's back flexing excessively. Changing the angle between the upper body and the leg allows far more range of motion than a wavy spine can manage. A wavy spine cannot support the rider's head steadily, so a bobbing head is generally considered a fault of seat. Sitting tall, elegantly, and looking beyond our horse's ears—even well to the horizon—helps keep our spine well-aligned.

Most seat recommendations that put the rider's legs away from the horse's side go along with at least decent use of the platform, since the rider has nothing else with which to activate the horse. I like having the additional use of more contact area, but contact below the knee is optional. Plenty of riders do without lower leg contact quite successfully as long as their legs aren't pushing their seat backward, against the horse's movement.

A sign of success in any aid is that it improves your stirrup connection. If you get lighter in your stirrups when you use an active seat your seat must be getting heavier, which is counter productive. Chances are that all got sorted out as you found the seat that worked for you and learned about using the horse's motion to your advantage in Chapter 3.

As your horse's trust of your seat and its physical ability to activate its back develops, the horse's back can follow ever more generous invitations from your platform for more movement. At this point, things change from the rider following the horse into the horse following the rider's seat, staying connected with it through the saddle as the rider moves bigger and more freely. It almost feels like you have rivets on your seatbones that lift the horse's back. This is a very neat sensation. And talk about being secure on a horse's back and in your stirrups! Nothing beats it.

A horse with a weak, stiff, or defensive back will likely give the rider a minimal swing to work with at first. It will not be capable of or willing to offer larger waves of motion along the topline, or not for many strides. This could be because of inexperience, tension, crookedness, history, soundness issues, unfitness, etc. How well a horse can follow a rider's seat is a reliable indicator of how well that horse's suppleness and strength are developing.

Supple and clear waves of motion all through a horse's spine from tail to ears tend to go along with the horse lengthening along its crest and its hind legs stepping well forward under its belly. What kind of head carriage that creates can vary considerably according to the horse's conformation and the needs of the job at the moment.

An active seat is not a digging seat. It doesn't make sense to try to convey that we want more and freer motion by poking or shoving on a horse's back, getting tight or heavy, or using less range of motion ourselves. Any sensible horse avoids these things, usually by tensing its back or, as the saying goes, running away from the rider's seat. It makes more sense to give the horse more room to move bigger, if that's what we want.

True, we can teach horses to go faster when we dig down with our seatbones, because we quit hurting their back when we get what we think we wanted. However, free, forward motion all through the horse's body is very different than just going faster, likely with very little play in the horse's topline. Make sure you really mean for the horse to tighten its back or even pull it downward when you use a digging seat, for that is what downward pressure on its back conveys to the horse. You cannot coerce a horse with your seat without creating resistance somewhere in the horse's gait mechanics.

Horses whose backs get pushed down have less forward swing in their hind legs. The forelegs then have to land earlier and shorter to catch some of the weight the hind legs would otherwise support by stepping well forward under the belly. Not surprisingly, gaits that do not allow a good forward swing of the hind leg are often rather flat and lacking in suspension. Horses whose backs are withdrawn also tend to shorten the crest of their neck, regardless of how high or low the horse may carry its head.

THE LIMITING SEAT

The third way we can use our seat is to limit the horse's motion. We will define the limiting seat to mean:

your platform not agreeing with the horse's motion.

Sometimes horses do things we don't want them to do. An easy way to tell them that is to make it uncomfortable for them to do that.

A limiting seat tells the horse, "No, I'm not going along with that."

One way to make a horse uncomfortable is to press down on their back with your platform, or maybe with one seatbone. This is one way to use a tushie-tuck and an intentionally heavy, tight, or bumpy platform.

In a limiting seat, the rider intentionally moves less than the horse moves. Again, timing is everything. A rider can only work against the horse's motion without creating tension somewhere in the horse and the rider, too. If a horse encounters an immobile seatbone when it activates its back (which is the same thing as activating its hind leg), one of two things can happen. Either the horse will reduce its activity level, or the rider will get launched off the horse's back to some degree. Sometimes to quite a large degree, like all the way to the ground. It happens.

We want to be careful that we aren't limiting the horse's motion at the wrong time. If the rider lost balance for a bit, stiffened and gripped onto the horse, that's a seat fault, rather than an aid. The question is whether what the horse felt was what we meant it to experience.

Another reason a rider's seat may limit the horse's motion is to try to get a halt or to slow down. A horse that is not very committed to its present activity level may well dribble to a halt or reduce its scope of motion if the rider does not at least follow the horse's motion passively. You can also train a horse to halt when you tighten up or lean back or push your feet forward or drop the reins on its neck or whatever signal you like. However, downward transitions and snappy halts, even (especially!) sliding stops, require a good deal of back and hind leg activity. So that is not a likely use of a limiting seat, although these movements may well call for a change in the rider's center of gravity to suggest and match the desired change in the horse's center of gravity. That's not the same as limiting the horse's motion.

The limiting seat has less to do with the rider leaning to the front or back, than with how much the platform agrees with the horse's motion. A rider can lean forward or backward without changing the swing of the platform much at all, or could keep the same vertical orientation and swing less. Which one counts as a limiting seat?

Pushing a seatbone into a horse's back might help keep a horse's back from arching stiffly while it prepares to buck, if you can also keep its head up and its feet moving forward. Shoving a seatbone into its back might tick the horse off even worse, though, especially if the saddle doesn't fit. Most of riding has to do with keeping the horse swinging well forward and therefore keeping the horse's back active, even in downward transitions, so the limiting seat isn't used that often. But, as we will see for all limiting aids, you'll probably want to switch from a limiting seat to active aids pretty quickly. As in human conversation, "No!" is usually best followed immediately by a request for what we do want.

The Unilateral Seat

The fourth way we can use our platform is unilaterally. We will define the unilateral seat as:

your platform redirecting the motion of the horse.

The unilateral seat says, "That will be fine if it goes over there."

The idea is to induce the horse to place its center of gravity and therefore feet somewhat to the side by shifting our weight somewhat to that side. It asks the horse's legs on one side to step toward that additional weight, just as we would likely step to the side if a backpack we are carrying shifts to the side. This shifts the combined centers of gravity of the horse and rider to the side. So, unilateral seat aids talk to the horse about things like turns, rollbacks, and pirouettes. They are also involved in related but more subtle matters of lateral balance (how much weight each lateral pair of legs is carrying), how the fore-hand and hindquarters are lined up, and lateral movements like half passes.

The trouble I commonly see in unilateral seat aids is a tendency for riders to curve their spine, which often pushes one seatbone down into the horse's back. It is quite possible to lean our shoulders over to one side by curving the spine and actually end up with more pressure or weight on the opposite seatbone or stirrup. Try it just sitting on a chair, and you will find that keeping your vertebrae aligned and changing your hip joint is a much more effective way to shift weight from one side of the platform to the other. It often works well to think of letting your knee(s) lead your hip joints in the desired direction. A sign of a good unilateral seat aid, like all seat and leg aids, is that it improves your stirrup connection.

Some riders shift a seatbone sideways, closer to the horse's spine. That can feel like there is more weight on it, when it is really a matter of the hips not staying level and the seatbone pressing sideways across the saddle. Some riders try to move their platform across the horse's back, thinking this will tell the horse to move sideways. The horse may figure this out, but the cross-ways action of the rider's seat will probably also convey to the horse not to swing its legs forward well. Horses moving forwards and sideways to any degree must swing the legs that are in the flight phase in front of the legs that are in the support phase (not quite true of the hind legs in spins), which takes a significant range of forward motion. Reducing the free play of the step when we are asking the hind leg to move bigger doesn't make much sense. A crossways-moving platform will also lift your whole leg on one side away from the stirrup, and probably twist your knee away from the horse, which conflicts with the idea that aids should improve your weight dropping into the stirrups.

Riders may also confuse the sensation of pulling a seatbone backward with letting more weight onto one side of the platform. They may feel increased pressure under one seatbone in this fault, too, but their leg on that side would again be pulled away from the stirrup, rather than having more weight dropped into that knee and stirrup. This fault often also goes along with the knee on that side turning away from the horse and the contact area rolling more toward the back of the thigh and calf.

The unilateral aid certainly uses a mobile platform that asks for more of a certain kind of motion. It can be used in combination with an active seat to get more forward motion in a certain direction. Think about how you want the center of gravity/oscillating water bag under the horse's spine to operate for the move you want to do, and you will know what to do with your unilateral seat, as well as all the other aids.

CHAPTER 8

Leg Aids that Work with Your Seat

All of us have probably had the experience of talking to someone and suddenly realizing we have "lost" them—that their attention has wandered . . . I believe this is the kind of experience our horses have when we just allow them to dawdle along.
—Jago

Nothing great was ever achieved without enthusiasm.
—Ralph Waldo Emerson

When we feel willing and eager, the gods join in.
—Aeschylus

After you have used your seat, the next aid to use is your leg. In fact, leg aids don't so much come after seat aids as flow from them and agree with them. Seat and leg aids are almost inseparable. The platform starts all communication to the horse, and leg aids can easily be thought of as extensions of seat aids, just as your contact area is an extension of your platform. As the saying goes, "The seat aid creates the leg aid."

A passive platform likely goes along with a passive contact area, and an active platform likely goes along with an active contact area. It is more likely that a mildly active seat plus a mildly active leg will produce what you want better than a very active seat and no leg, or lots of leg and a rigid seat. For one thing, our body parts are then all used in harmony, as they are designed to be used. We have seen that the motion of the rider's platform is going to influence the rider's leg anyway, unless we prevent that with muscular tension. Leg aids can be looked at as a way to agree with or amplify the seat aids, just like you can use two flutes to get more volume in a piece of music, rather than blowing harder on one flute.

Riders who rely on leg aids but at least make sure the horse's back and mouth are comfortable are building more cooperation than riders who use their seat, likely coercively, only after leg aids alone didn't get the job done. Using leg aids before seat aids very easily uncouples the rider's torso from their leg movement, typically by tightening around the top of the thigh. This can turn into a tight, limiting seat as a point of leverage to give "stronger" leg aids, a common form of clashing aids. In that vicious cycle, the stronger the leg aids, the more resistant the seat becomes. Horses are not likely to become lighter to the aids this way, unless they somehow get the message that the rider has ways to make them want to respond to leg aids even if their seat is not allowing more movement (read "whips and spurs").

Legs aids that start from tension cannot leave the horse more room to move, but somehow the horse is supposed to get the message to move bigger anyway. An active leg with a less mobile platform is your basic "the leg said 'go' but the seat said 'no'" communication. A horse can activate its legs somewhat without activating its back, but it isn't easy for them and doesn't allow the horse to use its full natural, athletic potential. Maybe this fault is so common because many riders are taught to use their leg ("Kick the nice horsie, honey!") before they are taught to use their seat. Under that sequence of training, riders may well learn without being taught that leg aids come first, or that seat aids are "difficult" or "advanced." Riders might learn to disassociate what their legs are doing from what their platform or the horse is doing. As we have seen, the things we learn without being taught can be both powerful and undetected.

Some time on the longe line checking out using the horse's motion to your advantage is one way around that; another good way is to hit the great outdoors on a reliable horse, and let it teach you what you need to know.

The Passive Leg

You may not be surprised to see the passive leg is defined as:

100 percent agreement of your contact area with the horse's motion.

Everything that goes for the passive seat aids applies to the passive leg. Passive leg aids agree with the horse's motion so well that there are no bips, pops, rubs, or friction anywhere along your contact area. A perfect passive leg wouldn't muss a hair on the horse's sides.

The passive leg says, "Yes, OK, carry on as is."

Like a passive platform, a passive leg lets your horse know you like what it is doing. It also contributes to your diagnostics of the horse's steps. We have seen that how the horse's body moves your contact area directly reflects what the horse's legs and body are doing, so a good passive leg adds to good diagnostics. If the horse generally experiences the rider's legs as staying quiet on its sides, it can easily recognize an aid as an aid, so a good passive leg leads to clear communication.

A good passive leg is equally important for horses that are dull to the leg and those that are oversensitive to it. Horses that are dull to the leg are likely in the habit of tuning out the bips, pops, and rubs the rider did not intend to convey to the horse. It may even have been corrected with bumps on its mouth or back, even if by mistake, for responding to those sensations as aids. In that case, the sensation we must convey to the horse must rise above the general level of rubbing and bipping the horse has learned to tune out, in order for an aid to register as an aid. This does not make for a horse that is light to the aids.

A horse who is nervous about a rider's legs in contact with its sides also needs a good passive leg. Many riders try to deal with such horses by keeping their legs extra far away from the horse. The rider's leg is eventually going to bop the horse by mistake, and everyone's worst expectations are fulfilled. Better that the horse knows where your legs are and learns that they are trustworthy and could become reliable guides.

The Active Leg

You may also not be surprised to see the active leg is defined as:

even more agreement of your contact area with the horse's motion.

An active leg says, "Yes! Give me more of what you are doing."

The platform largely uses the lift and drop of the horse's back for active seat aids, while the contact area uses mostly the left/right swing of the horse's barrel for active leg aids. As your horse swings your contact area, the horse is already giving you a good start on an active leg aid. You can let the horse's motion send your contact area on its way to dropping onto the horse's side more clearly. Voila! a tap with your calf. The horse's motion puts your leg in motion, rather than the rider contracting muscles to start it moving. The horse's motion will give us perfectly timed aids if we let it.

Leg aids that start with your heel or calf and push your knee up destabilize your seat and likely interfere with your platform motion, too. Leg aids that agree with your seat aids start from the top of your leg, right up in the hip joint, and travel down through your knee to the stirrup. Releasing your leg from the top of your thigh can drop your leg more onto the horse's side and into your stirrup. Aids like this secure our seat rather than disturb it, and avoid interfering with the horse's motion just when we wanted more of it. It works well to think of good leg aids more like seat corrections than as entirely separate leg motions.

Here is an experiment to get a sense of using the swing the horse already gives your leg to create a leg aid. Get a friend to help; stand on the lowest step of some stairs, or put a mounting block against a wall so you have something to touch a hand to and stabilize yourself. Stand with one foot along the edge and the other foot hanging free, with your hips level. With your leg hanging freely out of your hip socket, have your friend push a little on the front of your thighbone, say, about mid-thigh. Just a finger push is quite sufficient. Let your leg swing freely from your hip joint, so your torso is unaffected as your leg swings like a pendulum. If your hips or upper body start swinging, too, or your knee starts pointing outward, something is stuck or tight somewhere, probably in your hip socket, or maybe in your abdomen. Something could be stuck quite far away from your hip joint, like in a shoulder or your toes. Check it out.

The idea isn't to swing your leg as much as you can; the idea is to let it swing as much as the push it was given creates, no more and no less. Notice that if your thigh swings back far enough, it reaches the limit of the muscles that run along the front of your thigh. If your knee is unrestricted, your lower leg will then swing back even more than your thigh at that point. Let your leg swing until it comes to a rest all by itself.

Do this a few more times until your leg is swinging freely whenever your friend pushes it. Your friend can experiment with making your leg swing more or less by how much and when and where they nudge. Check out your other leg, too.

Once you have the idea of letting an outside influence swing your leg, have your friend nudge your leg into motion again, and use the momentum to exaggerate the last bit of swing. This almost whip-like effect is more like directing a limb release than a push or a punch. Next, compare tapping the face of the step by using the motion started by an outside source versus contracting leg muscles to set your leg in motion. If you want more oomph on any given swing, it works better to exaggerate the momentum of the last bit of swing the horse gives our legs than to put a lot of power into starting the motion ourselves. If the horse's movement starts our leg in motion, all we need to do is direct that motion. I believe this is similar to many martial arts techniques that seek to deliver the most power at the end of the movement of a limb that is already in motion.

You can moderate your timing to delay, quicken, or prolong how your leg uses the motion the horse gives it. This can suggest a different timing for the horse's leg play. These suggestions must still speak to specific feet, so it is a matter of timing and repeating aids to enforce them, rather than using forceful aids. Force has more to do with punishment than with being helpful.

An active leg is not a continuously squeezing leg. I believe people say "squeeze" to prevent rough aids like kicking, but riders can easily think squeezing means contracting their leg(s) on the horse's rib cage over many strides. If you want to lock a rider up, that'll do it! You can squeeze a horse for twenty strides, but that is still only one leg aid. There are times we use continuous pressure on a horse's side, but that cannot tell the horse you wanted more action from a particular foot or stride. I prefer the term "tap" to "squeeze," because it tends to keep the aid short and sweet. "Tap" invites repeated releases of any muscular tension that may have crept in and opens the door to using timing and the horse's motion rather than force or tension or contraction. You could think of it as very like the kind of tap you use on someone's shoulder to get their attention.

An active leg is not a rubbing leg or a twisting leg, which can get quite exciting if the rider is wearing spurs. With or without spurs, making little circles on the horse's sides with your calf or heel is bound to push your knee up at some point, and we know what that does to our contact area and platform. Nor do you need to twist the back of your leg onto the horse, turning your knee away from the saddle and likely interfering with your platform, too. Aids are always supposed to improve your seat, not disturb it.

An active leg invites more of the desired movement by using the horse's motion to start our leg into a swing. It is more like giving the horse permission to move bigger, rather than forcing them to do so. The horse will take you up on your invitation ninety-nine times out of a hundred. In my experience, the time it doesn't work is usually due to the horse's distraction, fatigue, or mistrust that the rider's seat or hands will be comfortable in a bigger stride, too.

An active leg is not a thumping leg. The active leg is either on the horse or more on the horse, not pulling your lower leg away from the horse's side to be able to thump it harder. What would you do if someone gigged you or even punched you in the ribs? That's a punishment, not an aid. As punishments go, it's not a very good one, anyway. It's hard to thump a horse's side without getting tight with your seat and jiggling your hand(s). The horse is very like-ly to be punished in the mouth and the back if it does move out as a result of getting its rib cage punched.

It doesn't make sense to enforce a correct leg aid by resorting to incorrect leg aids. If you feel the need to compel a horse to respond to a leg aid, it is much more sensible to leave your seat receptive and welcoming and add a tap with a whip to a nice leg aid. This may give the horse an opportunity to learn that responsiveness to nice aids can work out well for him, which the horse may not have had much reason to expect to date.

Riders also tend to believe that horses will respond to a tap with the whip, and that confidence in itself often removes tension and coercion from the rider's aids. The horse's improved responsiveness when a rider simply carries a whip often comes as much from the rider believing the horse will respond to aids and therefore giving better aids, than from the horse's actu-al fear of the whip.

Once again, we see that every aid, like every seat correction, starts from a muscle release. It's all much easier than some mysterious lower leg move-ment unrelated to our platform or the horse's steps, and perhaps subtle enough that it feels like the horse magically volunteered a swing that light-ened your platform and improved your stirrup connection. The line between a seat correction and an aid is thin indeed.

That creates a virtuous cycle in which leg aids improve your seat, instead of a vicious cycle in which seat and leg work against each other. If you get lighter in your stirrups when you use an active leg, something is wrong. Where must your weight go, if it isn't dropping into the stirrups while you are using an active leg? How is the horse likely to interpret that? What would prevent your weight from getting to the stirrups while you are using an active leg aid?

The sign of success that the horse responded to your active leg is that the horse gives your platform a bigger movement to use, setting up another vir-tuous cycle in which the horse's movement improves the rider's seat, in turn improving the horse's movement.

The Limiting Leg

You may not be surprised to see the limiting leg defined as:

your contact area not agreeing with the horse's motion.

Everything that applies to the limiting platform applies the limiting leg. In a limiting leg, the rider intentionally does not allow the horse's motion to move their contact area. A limiting leg says, "No, I'm going along with that."

Again, timing is everything. There is a limit to how much a rider can resist the horse's motion without creating tension somewhere both in the horse and the rider's entire seat. If a horse encounters an immobile leg when the rib cage is swinging toward that leg, one of two things can happen. The horse will reduce its activity level on that side, or the rider's leg will simply get pushed away from the horse's side.

You could think of the limiting leg as giving the horse less room to move. A limiting leg might be worth a try when a horse is drifting to the side to avoid a puddle on the bridle trail, which is basically the same physical action as running out on a jump or shying. Instead of staying lined up from tail to ears, the horse drifts to the side, often with one shoulder and his head pointing in opposite directions. If the horse starts drifting right, for example, we can try blocking the horse's barrel from moving too much to the right. The horse runs into our limiting right leg and voila! it might just straighten up, and over the puddle or jump or past the spooky thing we go.

Since the horse was not particularly keen on going through the puddle or over the jump or past the spooky thing to begin with, simply blocking the horse to the side with a limiting leg may not be enough to get the job done. Like all limiting aids, the limiting leg is a relatively weak aid. The horse may ignore or even push into the limiting leg. Serious hind leg activation might be needed to get the horse aligned and pushing itself forward again. A limiting leg is very likely to change to an active leg quite rapidly.

The difference between a limiting aid and an active aid is that limiting aids do not agree with something the horse started; active aids encourage something we do want. We can certainly tell horses "no, not that!" by not agreeing with their motion, but we also want to make sure the horse knows what we do want. Staying focused on what we do want is much more likely to get us exactly that. Who is in control of the conversation if we get stuck on reacting to everything the horse may offer that isn't what we want? Staying focused on what we do want, and any aspect of the horse's movement that is even a little bit more like what we want, keeps us more in control of the conversation.

Since most of riding has to do with keeping the horse's legs pushing off actively and swinging well forward (activating the horse's hind leg), the limiting leg aid isn't used that often and is rarely prolonged, but it might be just the right touch between a passive leg and an active leg. Again, we are talking about a spectrum, not an on/off switch.

We want to be careful that our contact area isn't limiting the horse's motion at the wrong time, perhaps because the rider lost balance and therefore free movement for a bit and unintentionally stiffened somewhere, especially in the legs. That can also crop up when riders jam their feet into the stirrups instead of releasing their legs to the stirrups from way up high in the legs. It is also very common for one of the rider's legs to be stiffer than the other in general. That's a seat fault rather than an aid, but a sensible horse may well get the idea it should not swing well on one side, or not swing at all, if one or both of the rider's legs are stiff.

The question is whether the horse felt what we meant it to feel. Did we convey the message we meant to send?

THE UNILATERAL LEG

We will define the unilateral leg as:

your contact area redirecting the horse's movement.

The unilateral leg says, "That will be fine if it goes over there."

The unilateral leg, most likely combined with a unilateral seat, seeks to shift the combined centers of gravity of the horse/rider unit to the side. That invites the horse to place its feet somewhat to the side, just as we would step to the side if the backpack we carry shifts to the side. So, unilateral leg aids are used to talk to the horse about things like turns and neat movements like rollbacks and lateral moves like half passes, as with the unilateral seat aid. The unilateral leg is commonly used behind the normal leg position (called "behind the girth") to tell the horse to shift its hindquarters to the side we want them to move toward or to prevent the hindquarters from swinging to the side we don't want them to move toward.

Some schools of thought use a leg in front of the girth or even forward on the shoulder to shift the forehand to the side. That may leave the horse with no information about what to do with the rest of its body, but a horse will easily learn what we mean by an aid in front of the girth, too.

The unilateral leg behind the girth, in harmony with leg and rein aids, can be used to orient the horse's hindquarters in relation to its forehand. If the horse isn't lined up well from tail to ears, it is not using both sides of its body equally well. The horse is said to be crooked, which is inefficient and will effect a horse's performance and eventually its health. There are those who say the horse should be straightened by orienting the forehand in front of the hindquarters, and those who say the hindquarters should be placed in line with the forehand. I would look at the way in which the horse isn't straight from tail to ears, and take it from there. This is discussed more in the section on "Lateral Flexion."

One trouble I commonly see in unilateral leg aids behind the girth is a tendency for riders to lift or twist the heel rather than extend the whole leg backward from the hip. This can get real exciting if the rider is wearing spurs.

There is an optical illusion to consider here, too. The sign of a soft ankle accepting the rider's weight is that the angle between the shin and top of the rider's foot closes as the rider's weight drops toward the stirrup. This is really what people mean when they call for low heels. If the stirrups are of a length to provide the support they are supposed to give, a closed ankle angle like this does place the rider's heel lower than the toes when the rider's leg is in the normal position. When the rider's lower leg is farther back, the sole of the boot may point down somewhat even when the angle between the rider's shin and the top of their foot is nicely closed and the rider's ankle is accepting weight well. The question is whether the ankle angle has opened or not. That's the angle to watch to see if the rider is dropping their weight toward the stirrup, regardless of where their lower leg is positioned. Pressing toes down or lifting heels will open that angle, whether the leg is under, in front of, or behind the girth, and says more than the angle of the sole of the rider's foot.

CHAPTER 9

Rein Aids that Work with Your Seat

It is hard not to act, but it is easy not to educate.
—Hans van Manen

Good hands are both steady and light. But how can a hand be steady
if the rider's seat is unsettled by the horse's movement? So, a light
and steady hand depends on the rider's light and steady seat.
—Gustav Steinbrecht

Nothing is so strong as real gentleness; nothing is so gentle as real strength.
—Anonymous, in *The Inner Athlete*, Dan Millman

If you guessed there are four ways to use the reins, you must have caught on to the scheme here. There will be a new twist here, though. We'll take a look at each of the four kinds of rein aids in a moment, but there are some basic issues about rein aids in general to discuss first. The same ideas will hold when we use bitless bridles like a hackamore, bosal, sidepull, or a halter and lead ropes, so you can substitute any of those whenever the word "bit" shows up.

First: rein aids cannot create forward movement; they can only direct it. Unbalancing a horse by pulling its head and neck to the side can get a sticky horse started, although not directly forward. Resorting to this means that your active seat and leg aids weren't working. Why not? Pulling a horse to the side to get it moving is like someone pulling your arm to get you to move,

A situation which more right rein isn't likely to help. What might have kept the horse better lined up from tail to ears and pointed the whole horse at the jump?

which is generally considered rude. An exception would be if someone pulls you out of the way of an oncoming bus.

Second: how do we know which rein aid to use? We have all had situations where the horse responded very differently to the same rein aid. Let's say your horse usually responds nicely to a right rein aid. But when he is trying to avoid a puddle of water or a jump by skittering to the left, even a very hard right rein doesn't necessarily make the horse move right to go straight over the puddle. It may even make the problem worse. Pulling a horse's head drastically to one side may only make them go the opposite way that much more.

The various rein aids are often defined by the movement the rider's hands should make. However, a different length of rein, the horse's head being higher or lower, or the horse looking one way instead of the other are just a few factors that could change how the horse experiences the bit even if the rider's hand movement is exactly the same. You can't reliably know what a horse will do according to a particular hand motion from the rider, or where the horse's head is pointing. There's more to it than that.

Will the real right rein aids please stand up?

Notice that this right rein aid looks a lot like the one in the first picture, but it has a very different result.

This right rein aid looks very different than the previous
photo, but seems to have a very similar effect on the horse.

For one thing, rein aids combine with the other aids to create a total
message to the horse. A bit of right rein along with an active left leg says
something different to the horse than the same rein aid combined with an
active right leg. A right rein aid combines differently with the rider's weight
shifting to the left rather than to the right, or forward or backward. Often
enough, riders do not feel how easily pulling on a rein may set up other
movements or tensions in their body, too. The horse may sensibly interpret
these combined movement or tensions as aids, too, while the rider remains
unaware of the total message the horse felt. Humans are very hand-oriented
by nature.

Another factor that can change how a rein aid turns out is what the
horse's feet are doing at the moment a rein aid is used. If the horse already has

a foot in the air, a rein aid can easily suggest that foot should step to the side or wait a bit before touching down. Or a horse may very effectively brace against a pulling rein if its feet are well planted.

The horse's alignment from tail to ears very much influences how rein aids turn out. We can see this easily with a simple experiment.

Imagine you have two lengths of 2 x 4 lumber, each about twelve inches long, butted up squarely against each other and pointing away from you on a table. Imagine you have a string attached to the left and right front corners of the block farther away from you. Pull both strings back and both blocks move back. What happens if you pull one string straight back? What if you pull one string a bit toward the side? What if you pull one string back or toward the side, but don't let the second block move backward? What if you only let one corner of the second block move?

Now, line the blocks up so they form a shallow V, or offset the blocks so they aren't quite square with each other, or try using blocks of different sizes. Pull both strings again, or just one of them, and try using them in various directions. The blocks may move back some, but the way the blocks are lined up is going to change, too. Double bonus questions: is there a way to use the strings to line the blocks up again? What's the quickest way to line the blocks up again? Triple bonus question: what if we used some materials more flexible than blocks of wood?

Similarly, how a horse is lined up from tail to ears will change how rein aids turn out. Kinks, tensions, and slack areas in the horse's alignment from tail to ears change how rein aids travel through the horse's body. In fact, these will change how all of our aids turn out, but this often shows up most obviously with rein aids. Bonus question: how would such misalignment change the horse's center of gravity?

So, how the horse experiences the rider as a whole and how the horse is arranged from tail to ears can explain why rein aids do or don't turn out the way we expect. Let's look at it from the horse's point of view.

The horse hasn't read any books that illustrate the various hand movements that define aids. All it knows is what it experiences from the bit. That will always be clear to the horse and that is what the horse will react to, so we can always define rein aids by how the horse experiences the bit. The real test of any rein aid is what the horse feels, rather than what your hand does.

How the horse experiences the bit must be the same as what the rider feels from the reins for most bits. Some bits use leverage (shanked bits) or pulley effects (gag bits) to multiply the effect of the rein aids. What feels like a couple ounces on the reins to the rider feels like much more than that on the horse's mouth. Riders who use bits like that need to be extra sensitive in their hands, or they might get surprised at the horse's reaction to what they thought was a light rein.

We riders can create the sensation we want the horse to feel from the bit as easily as we can tickle a kid with a feather. If there is one thing humans are designed to do well, it's to use our hands and tools. This is where we humans can really shine, using the very abilities that set us apart from unfingered animals.

Try this:

Hold the mouthpiece of a bit across the palm of your hand. Close your fingers over it, rather like the bit lies in the horse's mouth, and have someone hold the reins as if they were riding. You can close your eyes and tell what the person holding the reins is doing with their hand(s). Unless the reins are very loose, and probably even then, you can even feel if their hand simply tightens on a rein, much less actually moves a rein. So can your horse. Whether or not it reacts is a somewhat different question.

It's easy enough to tell if a rein is getting significantly tauter or looser. You can even tell just by feel if the person is making the rein a little loose, medium loose, or very loose. If you can't, either you have a lot of calluses on your hand, or the person holding the reins might be/could become a good rider. Leaving the bit steady while changing rein length is a very slick trick. It is also a high skill to be sensitive to small changes in a loose rein. I have great admiration for the many Western riders in particular who achieve that, and even seem to think it is a basic riding skill.

To get an idea of what riders can sense through the reins, see if the person holding the reins can tell without looking if you are holding the bit lightly in your hand, clamping down on it, or wiggling your fingers. As everyone's sensitivity develops, the person holding the reins can even tell if you are clamping or loosening your hand on one side of the bit or the other, or even if your back or your shoulder got tight. That's a lot like sensing how the horse is holding the bit in their mouth and how tension anywhere in the horse's body might show up through the reins.

Length of Rein and Contact

Horses can feel small changes in the rider's hands through a loose rein, and an alert and sensitive rider can identify how the bit sits in the horse's mouth through a loose rein. However, it is easier to feel what's going on through reins of a length that yields a direct feel of the bit. The rider can change how the bit feels in the horse's mouth more accurately and quickly through a shorter rein, although that need not be a tight rein at all. Shorter reins also transmit a rider's hands' mistakes just as accurately and quickly, though. Riding "on contact" can make the rider more aware of how the horse experiences the bit, but it also transmits hand mistakes more directly.

Riding with long reins is often an attempt to avoid the results of an uneducated hand or an unstable seat. Long reins do provide a bigger margin of error before the horse actually gets it in the mouth, but horses know if riders have messy hands with any rein length. It's tricky to take up slack reins smoothly, so rein aids given from long reins can be abrupt from the horse's point of view. It is tempting to snatch at longer reins, which can make for sharp rein aids alternating with loose reins. This reduces the good intention of using long reins to make a horse comfortable with the bit.

Riding with long reins can also reflect a basic belief that horses would not like contact with the bit. That may be true, but that must be something a horse was taught. It can also be harder for a rider to feel the horse's body's orientation toward the bit through long reins, so the rider who always uses long reins may not get much experience about how the horse's overall move-ment relates to the bit. Riding well on a loose or long rein is actually a high requirement on the rider. Riding with long reins (or no reins) can be a terrific display of mutual sensitivity and harmony. So can riding with contact.

The rider's hands, like our seat, have two jobs: they can receive informa-tion and they can transmit information. By far the more important job is to receive information.

How the rider holds the reins influences both how sensitive their hand can be and how easily their hand movements change the bit. A rein that runs from the horse's mouth under the little or ring finger (depending on how many reins the hand is holding), across the base of the rider's fingers, and then between the rider's thumb and base of the forefinger offers the best arrange-ment. Securing the rein between the thumb and forefinger leaves the other fingers free to move. Clamping the rein in a fist with all four fingers curled around it will be a tough, insensitive hand.

Riders who hold their thumbs away from their hand must be holding the reins with some or all of their fingers. This engages entirely different muscles all along the rider's arms, and even into the rider's back.

Try clenching your hands into fists. Notice which muscles in your hand and arm (and maybe even your belly) you use to tighten and loosen your fists. That's just like holding the reins or letting reins slip through your hand. Now try touching your thumbs on the bases of your forefingers, and lighten or tighten that connection as if you were letting reins slip through your thumb and finger or stopping them. That uses an entirely different set of muscles. More importantly, securing the reins between your thumb and forefinger leaves your fingers relaxed and free to move. This allows a smoother, softer, more responsive touch on the reins than when your fingers are busy holding the reins.

It is better to keep your fingertips lightly touching your palms, as long as that doesn't become a fist, rather than riding with open hands, with fingers somewhat extended. A hand with fingertips lightly touching the palm can open to soften and yield pressure on the rein quite easily. An open hand has nothing more to give. The rider with an open hand has to resort to larger, cruder, and therefore slower hand movements to soften and yield.

Riding with thumbs on top allows our freest, most relaxed rein aids, because no extra muscle tension twists our arm and wrist bones out of their natural alignment. Try this: let your arm hang loosely down at your side, and bend just your elbow to raise your hand. Your thumb ended up on top, with your hand coming fairly straight out of your arm and wrist. That is your most natural wrist alignment. Obviously, if we are well aligned ourselves, our hand will end up even and square if we do this experiment with both arms at the same time.

We are going to find out that how the horse carries the bit and orients its body toward it is a pretty good way to evaluate the horse's overall status. Since any seat problems are bound to also show up in our hands, horses might say much the same about people: how well we ride can be summed up by how good our hands are.

Accepting the Bit

There is a quality to what you feel through the reins. Simply picking up the reins can tell you a lot about the horse's personality and history. The horse's response can range from dullness to resentment to flinchiness to locking into a certain head carriage to dismissal to confrontation to eagerness to something akin to a handshake. Some horses are defensive about the bit, some have yielded the battle and have sworn never to touch a bit again, some are welcoming, or any attitude in between. This can be very subtle (a worried or welcoming look in the eyes) or overt (plunging the head down to take the rein out of your hands, snapping and clenching at the bit). There is a general feel of how comfortable the horse is about what it expects the rider's hand to do with the bit.

Accepting the bit means the horse is happy to go along with the bit's effects. Acceptance isn't certain head positions or neck and poll flexions. A horse that is content with the bit will be flexible in all of its joints, including the neck vertebrae and poll and jaw and even its hips and hocks and fetlocks. It will feel free to adopt the head carriage that best matches its overall balance. A horse that is not content with the bit may adopt a head carriage a rider imposes, but it will likely be a rigid and inelastic pose rather than a harmonization with the rest of its movement.

Many neck flexions and headsets riders insist on stem from riders assuming that horses automatically resist or avoid bits until they learn to hold their head and neck a particular way. Certainly the angle of the horse's profile and the position of the rider's hands determine the angle at which the bit will operate on the horse's mouth. But the various head and neck flexions and positions people get married to often have little to do with the horse welcoming the bit. Horses can easily be taught that bits hurt unless they do certain things that the rider prefers with their head and neck. That could be a certain form of acceptance, but it looks more like resignation to me.

Like whips and spurs, it isn't bits that hurt, it is how we use them. But let's get the verdict on how the horse you are riding feels about pressure from the bit, straight from the horse's mouth.

Try this:

Mount up, take up the reins and just stand. Any active gait will do, but this is easiest at the halt for most riders. Adjust your reins so they are even and just long enough that you have the lightest possible feel of the horse's mouth, or maybe an inch longer. Just so you know your hands aren't moving at all, put your hands down on either side of the withers in a place that maintains this very light feel of the horse's mouth. Keep your hands very still. Now, wait. Just wait. Waaaaiit . . . wait . . . keep waiting.

Before long, perhaps after a bit of fussing, your horse will start to relax its neck. You might want to slip the horse another inch or so of rein if it seems very worried. Little by little, the horse will release neck muscles and extend its crest until its mouth touches the bit. The horse may withdraw again, especially if the horse has been taught the rider thinks lightness means the horse should avoid the bit. Or the horse may plunge down hard on the bit, if touching the bit has been painful in the past. Don't grab back or jerk on the reins. Just keep waiting with absolutely steady (not tight) hands.

If the bit stays very, very steady, eventually the horse will relax its neck and comfortably touch the bit, at least for a moment. It is not unlike what we do to find out if something hot has cooled off yet. Keep your hands absolutely steady (not stiff or tight) and eventually the horse will, I promise, touch the bit more frequently and for longer periods of time. If your hands stay patiently steady, the horse will probably start thinking relaxing its neck would be nice . . . unless its teeth are a mess or the bit pinches, of course.

How do we know the horse is comfortable when it connects with the bit when we give it the chance to do that safely? If it weren't comfortable touching the bit, it wouldn't do it. There is nothing about this exercise that compels the horse to relax its neck and let its mouth touch the bit. The idea isn't to have the reins so short the horse can't avoid touching the bit if it doesn't want to, nor to have them so long the horse couldn't touch the bit however much its neck relaxed. The idea is to wait until the horse relaxes and releases its neck and probably its poll and back muscles. The horse doesn't have to keep its neck or anything else constrained to protect its mouth if the reins are steady and not too short.

If you wait very patiently, if your reins are even and your weight is square and equal on both sides of the horse's back and if the horse doesn't fall asleep, many horses will also volunteer a very square stand. They often come to find that standing squarely is the easiest way to carry a square, balanced rider. It distributes the combined weight of rider and horse proportionately over all four feet. It aligns the entire horse toward the bit, too.

You can do this bareback with a halter and ropes, if you have that kind of horse. In fact, it will probably work even better—and what does that tell us about what the horse "knows" about the bit? You can also easily feel how the horse's back muscles and neck muscles work together—or not.

You may be surprised how much weight some horses, even those that showed obvious reluctance to touch the bit at first, will voluntarily place on the bit if it is very, very steady and quiet for a period of time. You may be surprised how long many horses are quite content to let you carry their head for them, even though relaxing their neck muscles can put quite a bit of pressure on their own mouths.

I don't mean this to say that horses should put lots of weight in the rider's hands. But this does show that horses don't mind pressure on the bit per se as much as people often say (but rarely act as if) horses do. That doesn't mean that we get to mess with horses' mouths any way we want.

Try this too:

Once your horse has relaxed into the bit, tweak a rein a teeny little bit. Feel how much or how long of a finger clench it takes to put your horse on alert about its mouth. Maybe you get a pleasant elastic agreement, but maybe you get some tightening around the eyes, a stiffening or withdrawal somewhere in the horse's body, a head toss, a plunge down onto the bit, or a foot shuffle. You can almost hear it say, "Darn! Just when I was starting to think maybe that hand was trustworthy!"

Conclusions? One conclusion is that horses don't inherently mind some pressure on the bit *if they put it there*, whereas they may well be suspicious of us putting even light pressure on it. Horses will volunteer contact, sometimes even quite a frank pressure, with a very steady bit. But any connection with the bit has to be something they offer us, rather than something we impose on them. Contact we impose on the horse is very likely to produce resistance or evasion.

Another conclusion is that elastic, pleasant contact with the bit comes from a horse relaxing and releasing its neck and ultimately its entire topline. A horse that accepts the bit would even seek contact with it as a source of guidance. In that case, the horse would elongate to stay in touch with the bit if the rider offered it more rein. But horses are often very suspicious of even a finger twiddle on the part of the rider. If a horse is worried about simple contact, as shown by a reluctance to relax toward the bit, how can it be not be even more worried about rein aids that start with the rider putting pressure on the bit? Their first inclination is to withdraw and avoid the bit, which is different than elastically agreeing with the bit action. We *can accept* any amount of contact with the bit the horse voluntarily offers us without provoking resistance or evasion; we *cannot impose* any contact on the horse without calling forth some form of resistance or evasion.

Another conclusion is that horses will tell us many stories about what they expect from the bit. They are not usually stories of trust and comfort. I've ridden a few lucky, trusting horses, but the chances are higher that the horses we usually ride have little reason to trust how we handle bits, although they may be resigned to it. Positively accepting the bit and its effects is quite different than tolerating them. A horse that views the bit as a problem in any way is a very different ride than a horse whose experience has led it to believe the bit is another nice way to find out what the rider has in mind.

One of the basic challenges of riding is to convince the horse that we are worthy stewards of any device or action that can inflict pain. Sensitive hands are just the start. We need knowledgeable, trustworthy hands. Sensitive hands attached to an unbalanced rider cannot avoid making mistakes with the reins. The most sensitive hands in the world will still confuse the horse if they send messages that conflict with other aids. We need hands that are 100 percent clear about how the horse experiences the bit and how that combines with our other aids. We need hands that listen and are receptive more than they talk and lecture.

We can use the bit to mechanically move the horse's head, which is like pulling someone's arm to get them to do something. That may be necessary in an emergency—an emergency relating to the horse's well-being, that is, not an emergency related to our vanity—but it is basically not very nice. We can also teach the horse to do certain things with its head and neck based on bit signals. Teaching bit signals that have the horse's head and neck doing things separate them from the rest of the horse's body is like doing yoga only from the neck up.

Like any approach to aids as a set of signals, relying on trained responses to a favorite system of bit signals does work, to a point. However, viewing aids as signals or cues bypasses all the advantages that using the horse's forward motion already gives us.

We have seen that the horse's motion starts with the hind leg(s) pushing the body forward and that this motion travels forward along the horse's spine.

Every move the horse makes travels (hopefully) forward to the horse's mouth. If there's a bit in the horse's mouth, the horse's forward motion travels toward the bit. Using the horse's motion gives us everything we need to control the horse as a unit and to develop it gymnastically as a unit. We can use this motion from tail to ears toward the bit to our advantage a few different ways.

THE PASSIVE REIN

The first way we can use our hands or reins is passively. We will define the passive rein as:

100 percent agreement with how the horse moves toward the bit.

The passive rein is just a consistent (the same from stride to stride) and equal (the same on left and right side) connection between the rider's hand(s) and the horse's mouth. The horse would experience the passive rein as the bit staying still in its mouth, regardless of where its mouth is. The rider would experience the passive rein as a consistent feel in their hand(s) regardless of where the horse's head is or where their hands are.

The passive rein, like the other passive aids, says, "Yes, that's fine. Carry on as is."

The passive rein agrees with what the horse is doing with its head and neck, which in turn reflects what the rest of the horse's body is doing, unless we teach the horse to disconnect its head carriage from its overall balance. A passive rein is a good way to tell the horse we like the way its movement is oriented toward the bit. This says nothing about whether the reins are loose or taut, just that the feel in your hand(s) stays the same. Horses commonly ridden on loose reins, like many Western-style horses, would have a consistent loop in the rein. Horses commonly ridden with contact, like many English-style horses, would have a consistent tautness to the reins. The passive rein says nothing about how much weight "should" be in the reins, just that it would be consistent.

Like your passive seat and leg aids, passive rein aids provide you and your horse comfort, diagnostics, and clarity of communication.

A passive rein is comfortable for horse and rider. The horse isn't getting any bips and pops in the mouth, and the rider isn't getting his arms jerked out of the shoulder sockets.

A passive rein is highly diagnostic of what the horse is doing with the rest of its body. Tensions, suppleness, weakness, and strength throughout the horse's body will show up in its head and neck if the horse is allowed to use them freely. What you feel in your hand reflects what is happening everywhere else in the horse's body. If you have to let your hands drift forward to keep an even feel in the reins, it's a good bet the horse's body just got longer somewhere. If you have to let your hands drift backward, it's a good bet the horse's body just got shorter somewhere. If both hands have to move to keep the feel consistent, something changed pretty equally along both sides of the horse's body. If one hand has to move, something changed on one side. Your passive seat and leg give you the details of what may be lengthening or shortening.

The general sense of fluidity and elasticity or rigidity and inflexibility will also tell you if a horse lengthened or shortened because of muscle release and suppleness or because of resistance. A sense of having no connection would indicate evasion. These qualities will obviously also show up in the horse's gaits.

A passive hand makes for clearer communication with the horse. A horse used to some degree of bipping and popping or a constant grip from the rider's hands is likely to assume it should also ignore other bit pressures, too. Since pressure we didn't mean to put on the bit feels the same as pressure we intended in order to tell the horse something, the horse can't possibly distinguish between our mistakes and what we meant as aids. So our rein aids on such horses will have to be tougher or sharper or more prolonged than what the horse has learned it is best to ignore. A horse who knows that bit movement is always a communication the rider intended is going to attend to its mouth differently than one who knows some bit movements don't count.

As with all passive aids, we want to be sure that we are not agreeing inadvertently with something we don't actually want the horse to continue doing. This seems to crop up especially with regard to agreeing with a horse's misalignments. A rider who maintains a steady feel on both reins by adopting unlevel or unsquare hands can easily be agreeing with a horse that is quite misaligned. The horse may well get the idea that we want it to continue in its crookedness. That is quite different than aligning a horse's entire spine such that the horse voluntarily offers the rider's square and level hand(s) the same connection on both reins. Bonus question: what would it feel like if the rider maintained square and level hands despite a horse's misalignment from tail to ears? Double bonus question: how can the rider teach the horse to line up its entire body squarely with the bit? (Hint: what was the easiest way to line up the two blocks of lumber we experimented with earlier?)

THE ACTIVE REIN

We are going to define the active rein as:

even more agreement with how the horse moves toward the bit.

An active rein says, "Yes, I'd like more of that!"

Active rein aids can be used either with one rein or with both, depending on how you want the horse to experience the bit.

An active rein is not a matter of making the bit pull back on the horse's mouth. There is no denying that pulling reins can often slow or stop a horse and that many horses have been trained to slow or stop without rein aids at all. But if we are going to use rein aids, we have many more options than just more or less pulling on the horse's mouth to change how the horse experiences the bit.

How can the horse feel any change in the bit if we don't apply pressure on it? As always, we are going to use the horse's motion to our advantage.

When the horse pushes off with its hind leg, it extends its hind leg backward. The horse may well extend itself along its spine, too, but even if this forward movement along the spine is not very obvious, each vertebrae literally is pushed forward by the one behind it as the horse moves. This wave along the horse's spine is in addition to the head and neck movements that go along with the walk, canter, and gallop. The horse's spine has curves similar to ours, and this forward action along the horse's spine is a wave-like movement.

The horse's neck vertebrae are especially curvy and mobile. They can carry this wave action starting from the pelvis to the poll and from there to the horse's mouth. The neck may amplify that action, or it may act as a buffer between the body and the head. If the horse's neck is locked or kinked somewhere, it acts like a block or a diversion.

We can see an example of how the neck's potential buffering action might work out when a horse is standing rather forward in crossties, and it steps forward even more for some reason. Especially if the crossties are set high, the horse may end up pressing into the crossties with a very high head, its profile about parallel to the ground, its neck inverted with the crest shortened and likely its back hollowed down.

But let's say the crossties are set at about wither level (not a safe arrangement for crossties, but it makes the picture I am aiming for easier to imagine) and the horse steps forward to the limit of the crossties plus a bit. The horse would probably end up with its neck arched, its crest curved and lengthened, and the profile of its head about perpendicular to the ground. The horse may barely connect with the noseband of the halter, or it may press into it. The crossties, being inanimate, cannot have pulled on the horse's head. Nevertheless, the horse's body got closer to its nose.

In both cases, the horse's neck flexed to accommodate the horse's body moving forward. The first picture looks a lot like what happens when riders pull back and up with the reins, or when the horse expects that to happen. The second picture looks more comfortable to the horse and is much more like the kind of arrangement some riders spend lots of sweat and money to get their horse to do under saddle.

The horse may adopt a somewhat similar arched neck and perpendicular (or more) head profile when we press back on its nose or pull straight back on the halter, as we often do to get the horse to slow down or back up in our groundwork. There is a significant difference, though: the horse's nose got closer to its body, rather than the body approaching the nose. The neck compressed rather than lengthened and may well have flexed only in the upper third of the neck. I've noticed that doesn't reliably get the horse's feet to stop or move backward, though. If a horse doesn't want to stop or move its feet backward, it can just curl its neck more. Or the horse could immobilize its neck vertebrae. Tension along the horse's spine can change the vertebrae's buffering potential into something like a battering ram.

We can use this forward wave along the horse's spine and the horse's natural neck movements that go along with the hind leg action to change how the horse encounters the bit, similar to how it encountered the hypothetical crossties. These are the active rein aids, and there are two ways we can use the forward wave of the horse's movement toward the bit.

We are going to call the first way we can actively change how the horse experiences moving toward the bit the accepting active rein aid. This kind of active rein aid accepts the forward movement of the horse's body toward the bit.

In a passive rein, the rider would allow the horse to draw their hand(s) forward or let their hand(s) drift back however much was needed to maintain the feel of the rein in their hands and the feel of the bit the same in the horse's mouth. In an actively accepting rein, we change how the horse experiences the bit by letting the horse put pressure in our hand as the horse releases or extends its spine from tail to ears to mouth. We catch the forward motion of the horse's body toward its nose, so to speak. In an actively accepting rein aid, the horse's body moves forward toward the bit, rather than the bit moving backward toward the horse's body. We could use our hand(s) rather like the wither-high crossties, but hopefully with more cushion and sensitivity. Just as the crossties don't move to pull back on the horse's head if a horse steps forward to the limit of the crossties, the rider's hand doesn't pull backwards to create pressure on the bit.

Rather than the rider moving the bit backward in the horse's mouth to apply pressure, the horse moves toward the bit and the rider's hand *accepts pressure the horse puts on the bit*. One way to say this is that we allow the horse to step into our hand. Another way to say this is that the aids work from back to front (from the hindquarters to the forehand). The horse gives itself a rein aid, so to speak.

The rider's hand(s) can move with the natural gesture of the gait and wave of motion along the spine however is needed so the horse experiences the bit the way we want. You could think of it like a net catching the forward swing of the horse's center of gravity/oscillating bag of water.

The active accepting rein aid is a spectrum, not an on/off switch. We can accept some of the horse's movement toward the bit, or we can accept all of it. If the horse is sufficiently supple along its entire spine, accepting some of that forward movement brings the horse's hindquarters somewhat closer to its mouth. Some of the forward action converts into upward action, and the center of gravity shifts somewhat toward the hindquarters. Accepting all of the forward movement shifts the center of gravity even more toward the hindquarters, creating a halt with the hindquarters supporting a good part of the horse's weight.

Our hands may well move with the horse's motion even as we accept some of the weight/pressure the horse allows into the reins. Or we may not allow our hands to drift forward with the movement and neck movements at all and thus accept all of the pressure a horse may put on the bit.

An actively accepting rein aid does not add any pressure on the bit by moving our hands backward. We may well move our hands back as part of maintaining contact as the horse makes its natural head and neck movements, and we may well accept more movement in that direction if that is what we want to happen. That's different than just pulling back on reins. Bonus questions: what are the hind legs doing when the horse is drawing its head and neck back in its natural movement at the various phases of the various gaits? When might we want the horse to do more of that?

Losing a feel for the backswing of the horse's head and neck movements indicates a deadened hand just as much as a hand that is too tense to allow the forward swing. Horses don't like stepping toward a hand that is permanently stuck forward any more than they like a hand that is permanently held back. If you are riding with very long reins, you may have to bring your hand(s) back enough for the horse's motion to reach the bit before an active rein aid can really begin. However, horses do respond simply to changes in how loose rein(s) are, so a noticeable hand movement may not prove necessary even with long reins. Horses are well aware of less slack in the rein and respond accordingly.

The forward motion of the horse toward the bit might be a result of seat and leg aids, or natural enthusiasm from the horse. Even very lazy horses will occasionally move more frankly toward the bit, perhaps when they want to catch up with their buddies who got ahead of them on the trail. But an actively accepting rein aid has to have some movement from the horse to accept in the first place, if only a certain lengthening and release of tension from tail to ears, whether that action is created by the rider's seat and leg or volunteered by the horse. An actively accepting rein aid occurs as a result of the horse's motion traveling along the horse's spine. Now we know why the seat and legs aids came first in the list of aids and in the sequence of use. The rider's hands can only mold how we want the horse's forward motion to turn out.

For those who might be concerned that an accepting rein aid could "nail the horse to the bit," that it amounts to a fixed hand or pushing the horse forward and pulling back on the reins at the same time, please read on. Elasticity and responsiveness alone would prevent that, but there is also another guarantee: an actively accepting rein aid is never used alone.

The second way we can use an active rein is to yield to pressure the horse puts on the bit. The rider's hand cannot create forward motion, but an actively yielding rein aid can suggest to the horse that the rider would be happy to give the horse room to move forward. If we allow our fingers to soften or even allow our hand(s) to drift a bit more forward than we would for a passive rein, the horse might feel more than welcome to direct its activity toward the bit.

As the sayings goes, the only reason we take (accept) is so we can give (yield) again, or that we never take (accept) without giving back (yielding). Immediately. Without hesitation, whether or not we got what we asked for. We look for every opportunity to give back even more than we accepted.

Actively yielding rein aids are a great way to keep a rider's hands from getting grabby and tight in the first place. You can think of actively yielding rein aids as a thank you from the rider's hand for moving more freely, however subtle a muscle release may be. Common sense, social convention, and plenty of communication studies say that a prompt and sincere thank you is the best way to get more of what you want. Polite people even say thank you before they've gotten what they want. They include a thank you with their request instead of waiting for delivery. They say "Thanks!" for a partial delivery. They include a thank you for things people didn't even realize the person might be thankful for.

A timely and sincere thank you can be a terrific way to defuse a potential conflict and at least keep negotiations going. It can let the horse know the rider got the message that the horse would like more room to move, although we may not fully agree that is what we want. It can make the accepting rein aid more distinct to the horse. It can clear the board, so to speak, if a previous aid didn't work out very well. It can act like a pressure release valve.

We should be willing to look for reasons to thank our horses, since they were kind enough to let us on their backs in the first place. Tossing the reins on the horse's neck could be a form of a thank you for a nice ride in general, but we can do better than that. We can thank a horse for any step that is even vaguely more like what we wanted. Like many people who seldom get a word of appreciation, many horses seem surprised when they are first frequently thanked by a rider's hand. I have yet to meet one who didn't catch on rapidly and start looking for more ways to be thanked.

Actively yielding rein aids can be used any time, not just after an accepting rein aid. An actively yielding rein aid could be like a "thinking of you" greeting card, sent to keep in touch. Actively yielding rein aids are like the random acts of kindness recommended as a way to improve the world and reduce your own stress level. What a great way to practice that bit of wisdom!

Actively yielding rein aids can confirm and supplement active seat and leg aids. They convey to the horse that the rider will allow him room to lengthen his spine from his tail right to the ears and beyond in response to active seat and leg aids. By encouraging a release all along the horse's spine, a yielding rein aid allows the horse's feet to do what the rider's seat and legs ask the horse to do.

Actively accepting rein aids may create a momentary compression of the horse's spine from tail to ears as the rider catches the horse's forward motion traveling toward the bit. That compression is immediately released by the prompt, actively yielding rein aid that always follows an actively accepting rein aid. The release is really what we are after, in fact. Without this release, we would be asking the horse to be rigid along its spine, and we would teach the horse to barge onto the bit with a stiff back and neck. That would not be of gymnastic benefit, nor would it be comfortable for horse or rider.

Instead, we want the horse to develop its ability to use its entire topline like a buffer. This ripple along the horse's spine and all the muscles around it may be so minute as to be barely perceptible to begin with. But if you want to develop a strong, springy back under you, this release will prove indispensable for suppling and strengthening the topline muscles that operate the rest of the horse's body. Without this release, as subtle as it often is, forward motion toward an unyielding bit could turn the extra activity we ask for into tension and rigidity rather than freedom and elasticity. Lest the neck's and even the entire spine's buffering potential be overtaxed and call forth resistance, we must be sure not to accept more pressure on the horse's mouth than the horse can comfortably and resiliently adapt to throughout its body.

This forward wave of motion toward the bit can develop into the kind of brilliance and dexterity at all variations of all gaits that can only come from a well-developed topline. It can develop into the kind of halt that makes you think of bold soldiers snapping to a salute and ready for the next move. It is a dream to ride. It is close to impossible *not* to sit beautifully on a back like that.

If the horse doesn't have much forward motion toward the bit to begin with, this is like pushing a string at first. Not moving well forward toward the bit could originate from laziness or from rigidity somewhere along the spine, even if the horse is moving energetically. Even then, perhaps especially then, actively yielding rein aids can be worth gold and diamonds and music from heaven. Actively yielding rein aids are especially needed with horses who are sticky about leg aids, jammed onto the bit, tense anywhere in their body, or have reason to think rider's hands are grabby or tight.

As the horse's spine gains in suppleness and strength, it will be comfortable with ever-larger waves of motion along its topline. A sure sign that the horse is gaining suppleness and strength in its topline is how elastically the horse's back, neck, and poll can transmit the body's forward motion toward the bit. Some people call this "accepting the bit" or even "throughness," although these are not entirely the same thing. "Throughness" is a currently trendy translation of the German word *durchlaessigkeit*, which literally translated means "let-throughed-ness." There is more to *durchlaessigkeit* than this, but it does give a sense of how action can travel freely along the horse's spine as well under saddle as it does when the horse is at liberty.

Any joint, especially between vertebrae, that is slack or stiff or out of alignment will diminish, stop, or misdirect this wave. A sure sign that the work we are demanding exceeds the horse's current suppleness and strength is the horse getting defensive anywhere along the spine in response to an active accepting/yielding aid cycle under good forward motion. This could show up as a tossing head, an opening mouth, a tongue hanging out, a dry mouth, jaws crossing, the head's profile coming behind the vertical, or the neck (and the whole spine, really) flexing unequally along its length. About three vertebrae behind the poll is a popular spot for horses to flex too much, while leaving the neck vertebrae closest to the horse's barrel or in the poll area out of play or even locked. We may also see propping legs, reduced scope in the stride, lagging response to activating aids, the hindquarters sliding off to the side, shoulders popping to the side, or anything but springy flexion and extension equally all along both sides of the horse's spine toward its ears and right on through to the horse's mouth. Better by far is gradually to develop elasticity evenly throughout the horse's body.

Both accepting and yielding active rein aids are quick, and we see again that timing is everything. Active rein aids, both accepting and yielding, may well be repeated, but they are never prolonged. Active rein aids must speak to specific phases of the steps and even to phases of specific feet, so active rein aids cannot last long at all. It is entirely possible for a few actively accepting/ yielding rein aid cycles to happen within one stride. The message to a particular foot within a particular stride could be: "wait a bit right there—thanks!— and wait a bit right here—thanks!—that's enough—thanks!"

Big hand movements take too long to hold that kind of conversation.

Most active reins aids are a matter of movement within the rider's hand(s). They would not easily be seen except by how they influence the horse. They are a rather intimate conversation between the horse and the rider.

A pretty emphatic active rein aid could be actual finger movements within the hand movements that follow a horse's head and neck gestures. Like very strong leg aids, much more than that starts to move into the category of punishments rather than aids. It is always better to reinforce aids by making them quicker before we consider whether making them harder is likely to work. After all, saying something louder or with a sharper tone of voice doesn't help anyone understand what you are saying, unless the problem really was that they couldn't hear you. Calm, clear repetition is more likely to gain the horse's understanding and cooperation.

Some horses will put a lot of pressure on the rider's hands at times. Especially if the horse stiffens its neck and probably its back, it can take a strong back on the rider's part not to give in to that pressure and thus teach the horse that lugging on the bit gets the rider to yield the reins. Many riders simply reach for a bit that inflicts more pain than the horse is willing to challenge but requires no more effort on the rider's part. Far better to restore the horse's flexibility and balance and its trust in the rider's aids.

A strong horse with tremendous forward spirit may need a stronger bit to be able to capture all that power, much like a large truck or a fast car needs heavier duty brakes than a go-cart needs. Some horses can throw an awful lot of weight and power toward the bit and still be elastic and supple. However, that is different than selecting a bit for its pain potential and its ability to convince a horse to avoid it, at least until the horse gets accustomed to that level of pain and an even sharper bit must be found. The question is whether the horse remains elastic in its rein responses, which has far more to do with how riders use bits than with the kinds of bit used. Horses that can go reliably in softer and softer bits, as well as horses that still trust their rider even if a sharper bit is used, are both signs of success.

But the actual hand movements that change how the horse experiences the bit might still be most effective by staying small and quick even when the horse is bracing on the bit. It's difficult to brace against a moving object.

If you are absolutely sure you really need to punish a horse, there are usually lots of better ways to do that than wapping them in the mouth with the bit. Such a thing would be an absolute last resort, used for things like horses attacking people or running toward the edge of a cliff and such. Something usually has been going wrong for some time before such dramatic situations arise.

One exception to using active rein aids quickly could be a very obvious and prolonged yielding action to assuage a horse's concern that their mouth is going to get grabbed. An exaggerated yield is akin to an apology for having grabbed too much, or for other riders having grabbed too much in the past. It is also a necessary prelude to seeing how the horse reacts when the rider re-establishes contact that can speak volumes.

So, we can actively accept pressure the horse offers to put on the bit as it extends toward it, or we can actively yield to pressure the horse offers to put on the bit. We can accept or yield as much of the pressure a horse may offer to put on the bit as is necessary to achieve our desired outcome. The active rein aids mold the horse's movement toward the bit according to how we want to influence the motion of horse's center of gravity.

If the active seat and leg are verbs, the rein aids are adverbs. The active seat and leg say "go," and the active rein aids say "go like this."

The Limiting Rein

We will define the limiting rein as:

disagreeing with how the horse moves toward the bit.

A limiting rein aid says, "No, I'm not going along with that."

One reason we might disagree with what the horse is doing with the bit is that the horse is being bad. No doubt the horse has its reasons, but there are times when a firm "no" is a valid part of the conversation. Simply setting your hand in place is a good way to convey this. Jerking on one or both reins is not an aid. That doesn't say "no" to a horse as much as it says "I can make you feel pain." Most horses already know this and don't need to be reminded except in extreme circumstances.

It won't be long into your riding career before you will have an opportunity to see when a limiting rein might be useful. There you are, perhaps just mounted up a few minutes ago. You could swear you didn't so much as twiddle the reins in your hands while you were adjusting them, and the horse dropped its head and just about took the reins out of your hands. If you managed to hang on to the reins, you are sprawling over the horse's neck. Some ponies are really good at this, especially when there is grass nearby.

Or you run across a horse with whom holding the reins is as good as wrapping the reins around a lamppost. Those guys can make you wonder where anyone got the idea horses' mouths are so sensitive. It is easy to assume that isn't true for horses who seem more than willing to jam themselves onto the bit so hard.

And then there are the rubber-necked horses. Pull on one rein as you like, the horse goes the other way. You can have such horses' nosed pulled around about to your knee, and they will still go the opposite direction.

As you can see, these are not generally signs that things are going well. Any of these situations might call for not agreeing with what the horse is doing.

In the first case, when the horse plunges its head suddenly onto the bit as you pick up the reins, it might be worthwhile to let the horse teach itself it is being rude—and then make sure to teach it the worries that may have prompted the rudeness are a thing of the past. You can be sure that snapping the bit after it has half-dragged you out of the saddle will only confirm the reason the horse thinks riders are not to be trusted with reins. Sharper bits will have the same effect, of course, if the idea for using a sharper bit is to be able to inflict more pain to try to get the horse to stop this annoying habit. If you want to teach the horse how to tolerate more pain, using a sharper bit is the way to go about it, all right. Restoring the horse's original sensitivity would take a different approach.

We will never win a muscle battle with a horse, but we can use leverage. One way to deal with a horse that plunges suddenly down on the bit to pull the reins out of the rider's hands is to hold one rein at a normal length in a hand braced against the horse's neck . . . but let the other rein slip. A horse cannot easily tug very hard on just one rein. The horse will also have a chance to learn that the rider's hands are not always going to have a death grip on the reins, which is what such horses are probably trying to take care of in the first place. The horse may even discover that it can release the muscles in one side of its neck very pleasantly, so be sure you let the other rein slip at times, too, so the horse can discover this for both sides of its neck.

In the case of a horse boring or lugging at the bit, ask yourself: why is the horse so heavy in your hands? It may be a result of exhaustion, imbalance, or defensiveness. A very tired horse may well hang in the rider's hands, and it may be a good idea to give the horse the support it needs. That would show up at the end of a long work and wouldn't be the horse's regular way of going about things. It will go away when the horse is refreshed.

A horse may be quite imbalanced and need some support until you help it figure out how to support its center of gravity better by itself. Just like in dancing, there are times you hope your dance partner hangs on! Teaching the horse to solve its balance problems other than using the rider as "the fifth leg" is more to the point than punishing the horse's mouth. Hard contact is a symptom of a more basic problem elsewhere in the horse's mechanism. A rigid mouth usually goes along with a rigid neck and back. Activate the horse's back and its ability to support the freely swinging center of gravity with freely swinging limbs that a horse considers a normal way of moving, and the mouth problems tend to disappear. Mouth problems tend to disappear at the same rate as the horse's gymnastic development progresses.

Some horses that are concerned about what riders do with bits may well hang heavily and stiffly on the rider's hands, much like we hold or squeeze a finger that hurts. Causing more pain by jerking the horse's head up or going to a sharper bit is likely just to strengthen the muscles the horse is already using for this kind of resistance, creating a vicious cycle. Some horses have figured out that they can win pulling contests with most riders. If they just don't give up, the rider's arms or resolve will give up first. If you decide it is time to show a horse that isn't true, the trick is to use your back rather than your arms. Showing the horse that using their own back gains them comfort through their whole body as well as their mouths also restores their natural agility.

You can use a pulling horse's own strength to your advantage by letting them pull you into the saddle, rather than pulling you out of it. You can even let this help you create the seat and leg aids that in turn help the horse unlock the muscles that have it "nailed to the bit," as discussed under the active rein aids. If the horse discovers releasing the muscles it has been using to barge through the bit eases everything, including the constant pressure on its mouth, the horse might decide you had a pretty good idea. You have probably already realized that some yielding rein aids, likely with just one rein, would make a great sauce for that recipe. A horse can't lug on something that isn't rigid. Certainly activating the horse's back and the barrel's left/right swing instead of letting the horse continue to use its spine like a battering ram will help. We see again the potential for metronome-like aids instead of gas-pedal-like aids, and why limiting aids usually turn into active aids.

All three examples—the horse that jerks the reins out of the rider's hands, the horse that is heavy in the rider's hands, and the rubber-necked horse—are the same in one very significant way: the horse is following its center of gravity, and that will always override aids which try to work outside the laws of Nature. The rubber-necked horse is different in one very significant way. In the first two examples, the horse's center of gravity is being propelled forward toward the horse's head, which has the seeds of success inherent in it. In the third example, the horse's center of gravity is aiming more to the side. The rubber-necked horse is doing very different things with one side of its body than the other.

The horse's body is going to follow its center of gravity, regardless of the rein aids riders apply. With a rubber-necked horse, the direction the horse's center of gravity is oriented is not necessarily the same as the direction the horse's head is pointing. Pulling a rein may well just exaggerate the difference.

In that situation, the basic difficulty is that the horse is not lined up from tail to ears. The horse's motion can travel well along a straight or an evenly curved spine, just like a train can travel a straight or an evenly curved track. But the horse's movement cannot travel well along a misaligned spine any more than a train can travel a track that has a V in it. A spine with one big kink in it (usually in the neck, often just in front of the shoulders) instead being straight or having a smooth arc from tail to ears, is not a spine that will transmit movement or aids well. As the saying goes, the aids stop wherever the kink is.

A limiting rein aid on the side toward which the horse's center of gravity is drifting can help misalignments by limiting how far the horse's neck and shoulder can get out of alignment with the rest of its body. A limiting rein aid by itself won't fix the problem, but it could prevent it from getting worse. A limiting rein can help limit misalignments.

As with all limiting aids, we want to get to the part of the conversation that tells the horse what we *do* want as quickly as possible. Once a problem is contained, and even as we work on containing it, it is always best for the rider to make the first suggestion about what a good solution might be. We can control the conversation better when we get to pick the topic. Just as with limiting leg aids, we very likely to switch to active aids as soon as the "no" part of the conversation has been said, if it really needs to be said at all. The solution to a rubber-necking horse is to get the horse to realign and actively push its body forward again. So, we may well use a limiting rein aid and leg aid on one side of the horse to limit how far out of alignment the horse gets and move on to an active seat and leg on that side. An actively yielding rein and active seat and leg aids on the other side can contribute to the message to "line

Not much is aimed where the rider means to go. What could the rider do to get everything lined up for the jump?

up and move on." The emphasis of each kind of aid may well vary from stride to stride to meet the needs of each step.

Unilateral Rein Aids

We can define unilateral rein aids as:

redirecting how the horse moves toward the bit.

Unilateral rein aids say, "That would be fine if it went over there."

There are a few ways we can redirect the horse's movement toward the bit, which is to say, direct its movement to the side. We can move the bit toward the direction we want the horse's center of gravity to move. You can think of this as opening a door to allow the center of gravity/oscillating bag of water more room to swing in that direction. This is called an opening or leading rein.

Or one hand can move the rein toward the horse's neck on the side opposite the direction we want the horse's center of gravity to go, perhaps even pressing the rein on their neck. You can think of this as nudging the horse's center of gravity/oscillating bag of water in the direction we want it to go. This is called neck reining or the bearing rein.

Sometimes we can do both of these at the same time. That's basically what happens when we hold both reins with one hand, or when two hands stay still in relation to each other, and we move them to one side or the other.

These aids have to do with sideways movement, which can mean turns, lateral movements, or refining the direction in which the horse's center of gravity is swinging. This might also be useful when we want to orient the

One nice thing about neck reining is that they use no backward action. Horses are often very willing to stretch toward the bit on the outside when the aids are used like this.

horse's forehand certain ways in front of the hindquarters, assuming we are not mistaking that for putting a kink in the horse's spine. As always, we will be using seat and leg aids that agree with the unilateral aids, so the horse gets a complete message, not just its nose pointed somewhere. This is discussed more in the section about lateral flexion.

CHAPTER 10

Two More Aids, and How to Tell if Your Aids Are Working

Ending up with a good horse always takes some thought. . . .
Ending up with a bad one takes no thought at all.
—Mark Rashid

To teach the horse faults we need merely be unobservant.
—Henry Wynmalen

Let your "yes" be "yes" and your "no" be "no."
—Matthew 5:37

We have seen how we can use our own physical connections with the horse to send the messages we want to send by controlling how the horse physically experiences us as riders and how that works with or against their movement. However, there are two more categories of aids we can use. They generally confirm or emphasize what we intend to communicate by the way we ride.

THE VOICE

It is quite possible to teach horses what we think words mean, like walk, trot, canter, whoa, stand still, and so forth, and various sounds like whistling or clucking or grain rattling in a bucket or the crinkles of a plastic bag. Horses learn whatever words and signals we teach them. As far as they are concerned, we could say "rutabaga" when we want them to canter. But they will learn what we mean by various words and sounds, to the point that I can't say or whisper the word "canter" in a side conversation while longeing Council Hill unless I do want her to canter. I can't even spell it without her making that transition. I'd say that means horses can learn words and that more than one word or sequence of sounds can refer to a particular thing. That's handy when you are importing horses.

The most important word you can teach a horse is "whoa" or "ho," or some word that means "all four feet on the ground, right now." The easiest time to take care of this is when the horse is first halter broken. Unfortunately, people can get sloppy about this and resort to physically stopping the horse instead of enforcing the word command.

How we use our voices and equipment with horses in groundwork is a great way to reveal a lot of patterns we get into with horses. Groundwork can explain much about possible sources of miscommunication under saddle, if we don't leave those lessons on the ground.

I see a lot of double cueing in groundwork, which means using the word we want the horse to learn along with using a gesture. This could be stopping or moving ourselves, or adding a tap with the whip or a tug on the leadline at the same time we say the command to go or to stop. In that case, the horse may very logically decide that only the word plus the gesture counts as the real command. The horse may well conclude the word or the gesture alone doesn't mean anything.

It is altogether different to speak a command and then enforce it (which means praise as much as it means punish). In that case, the horse learns to respond to the word alone, rather than the word plus a gesture. Trainers and handlers need to be clear on the difference between the cue (the word we want to teach the horse) and the enforcer (the reward or penalty), as John Lyons puts it, or the horse will not learn what we think we are teaching them. We cannot then be surprised when the horse responds in ways we did not think we had taught them.

A common example of double cueing in longeing is when the handler constantly flips the whip or line at the horse to keep it going. It is one thing to correct the horse if it slows down without being asked to do that. It is another thing to flip the rope or whip at the horse all the time just to maintain a gait. If you teach the horse that it should carry on what it is doing only while you are flipping the rope or whip, then that is what it will learn. In that case, not flipping the rope or whip could logically mean "stop doing what you are doing." It also means that we have to flip the rope or whip at the horse even harder or differently to indicate a change.

This isn't the worst thing in the world, but you may inadvertently teach the horse that it must be constantly cued to keep moving and that it shouldn't keep going if you are not actively cueing it every stride. If that is not how you want things to go later, the horse will have something new to figure out then, something you may not have realized might be a question for them. We could easily mistake this for laziness, when in fact we are the ones who taught the horse that pattern.

Interestingly, most double cueing in groundwork happens with threatening-type enforcers like whips and rarely with encouraging-type enforcers like praise. Much of our praise for the horse, especially in groundwork, comes from our voice, and we must necessarily speak the cue before we can speak the praise, so encouraging-type enforcers like words of praise are virtually impossible to double cue. The same is true for a voiced correction, of course, so one way to break the double-cueing habit with whips and such is to make a rule that you can't use equipment to enforce a command unless it accompanies a voice correction, not a voice command.

People also use "whoa" to mean both "slow down" and "stop," which I think causes unnecessary confusion for the horse. If "whoa" doesn't really mean "stop," what do you use for "stop"? Slowing down enough does end up in a stop, and horses seem to figure us out. I suppose they learn to take things in context, but it does plant the seeds for possible miscommunications. I would make sure there was some word that means "stop, immediately" and means nothing else, for that could save someone's neck someday in an emergency. I reserve "whoa" for an immediate halt, and "wait" for slowing down.

Horses definitely respond to tone of voice as well as specific words. Your tone of voice is like the music that goes with the lyrics. In fact, tone of voice often trumps the actual word used. Even a horse that is well trained to voice commands can get confused when the same word is used with a different tone of voice. Saying "canter" in a very low, calming way when you usually use a bit of lilt to your voice for the canter command may well change how a horse performs the command. The horse might well decide that's different enough to count as a new word it doesn't know. I have often seen horses misinterpret a very enthusiastic trot command for a canter command, especially if the handler was not aware that the horse was already at a pretty active or an irregular trot for that horse. It's easiest to be consistent if our tone of voice matches what you want to happen—rather lilting for upward transitions, rather drawn out for downward transition—with consideration for the horse's personality and mood of the moment. Nervous horses may even take an enthusiastic lilt as a threat.

Your tone of voice speaks to the horse's emotional or moral condition, whether or not what you say includes words the horse knows. You can speak encouragingly, calmly, enthusiastically, crossly, jokingly, or anything else, as you feel will help the conversation along.

The rhythm of how you say things also counts, to the point that it is quite possible to speak to a specific foot rather than just to name the gait we want. This can be essential to improving the quality of gait. A cluck when the horse is about to push off with a particular hind leg may do more to open up its stride with good rhythm, instead of just generally speeding up, perhaps with an irregular rhythm. We generally get what we ask for.

A real pet peeve I have is multiple requests used to get a single response from a horse, and this shows up in a heartbeat in longeing. Once a horse knows a command, it is a bad idea to ask more than once without some enforcement of one single command. Enforcement means reward just as much as punishment, of course, but our patterns are often most glaringly obvious regarding a command not being obeyed. Unless the horse has a darn good reason not to at least make a prompt try, it is far better to enforce one command, and then repeat it if necessary, than to ask three and four times for the same thing before we let the horse know it isn't getting the job done. The horse will learn what we teach it. You can teach it either that only the third or fourth command really counts, or you can teach it that one command is sufficient to at least get started on the job.

Giving multiple commands tends to go along with using the same word (or aid) as a command and as a threat (trot—trot!—TROT!!). This tends either to get horses flinchy about the command, or not to believe the command counts until you are screaming (or kicking). This usually has to do with adding crossness or even anger to unfulfilled commands. An angry command is not as effective as a reasonably-voice command enforced with a show of the whip, perhaps. It is far better to ask once and enforce (trot—no trotting happening—show the whip) than to ask again and again (trot—trot—trot!—show the whip). Giving multiple commands without getting results (also known as nagging) is the quickest way to dull a horse I can think of. A better approach is one request, one response. Ask once and tell the horse whether it is doing its part or not. Repeat as needed.

It is certainly true that horses respond to body language as well as spoken language, often to a much greater extent than we realize. Indeed, it is very common to see horses responding more accurately to body language than to voice. If you are wondering if that's true for your horse, try leading your horse as usual, say the word "whoa," and keep walking. Next, try leading your horse as usual, don't say anything, and stop walking. What your horse does tells you what it actually has learned, which may not be at all what we thought we had taught them.

This is a minor example of how sensitive horses are to body language. I have seen sensitive horses hesitate to approach people they normally like if that person is in a bad mood or nervous, even if the person denies anything is wrong (usually rather curtly).

Whatever patterns you use regarding voice commands and general body language on the ground will likely also show up in your aids in the saddle. Check it out.

Auxiliary Aids

Auxiliary aids are all the mechanical devices available, like whips, spurs, martingales, tight or special nosebands, special bits, special rein devices, chains, the many and various devices to keep horse's heads or mouths in certain places, and other admissions of defeat.

I am even tempted to put some saddle pads in this category. Certainly some chemicals could be counted here, too: anything from some ginger under a tail or soaking sore legs in icy water just before a race, to performance-enhancing drugs, starting with aspirin and some herbs.

Somewhere along the line we can get the idea that the way to control movement is to stop it, limit it, counter it, or micromanage it. We can instead direct it and use it to our advantage. We can look for some part of each stride that has something about it that is a little bit more like what we want to happen. We may as well concentrate on amplifying what we do want than getting hung up on stopping what we don't want. Most mechanical devices are about stopping what we don't want, or with eradicating unwanted symptoms of horses' normal and logical physical responses to our riding.

Since we can't really outmuscle a horse, approaching riding as a power game tends to have humans reaching for sharp bits, spurs, and whips to overpower the horse, or at least have them ready to hand should the need arise. I'm OK with being ready for that in theory, but for the most part it isn't necessary.

I am the first to let a horse know that trying to use its power against me when I make a reasonable demand will not work out pleasantly for them. A more dominant member of the herd would do the same. Horses mostly work out these dominance issues among themselves without causing each other pain, although the threat of doing that is certainly there. Granted, there are horses that are just nasty tempered, confrontational, and aggressive. Those are often the horses that can end up being absolute tigers about getting a job done, if we can direct that power instead of trying to uproot it. Trying to uproot it usually just teaches them how to fight better.

I have also found that most horses (once they are past their "teenage phase" at about two or three years old) don't offer that kind of behavior toward people without reason. Most horses are remarkably generous, if you start looking at what their physical experience of riding probably is. They become less generous when they are in pain, confused, scared, or taken for granted, just like people do. A horse may have reason to believe the best defense is a good offense or that a person or all people deserve reprisal, and it's his job to hand it out. By the time any of this comes out in a full-blown battle, there have surely been far more subtle indications of trouble that we overlooked. Since we are supposed to be the smart ones in the party, the blame for that rightly lies on the human.

In my experience, riders simply didn't realize any problems were brewing, being rather unaware of low-level resistances/communications. Most riders are not so tough on their horse that the horse figures it's worth getting into a fight, but neither are we always making their job as easy to understand and perform as we could. Strong aids do not compensate for poorly timed or conflicting aids, for example. We will never be perfect at this all the time, which most horses can deal with quite easily, but we can always be open to improvement, for which the horse will give us everything it can.

Whenever you are considering using some special device, first ask yourself why you need it. If the horse isn't getting the message you intend to send without adding something more than what you were born with, why is that? If the horse is getting the message but isn't cooperating with it, why is that? If you can honestly say that some mechanical device can get the job done better than you can yourself, consider whether there is something you have yet to discover about riding before you decide for sure that the horse is the one that doesn't "get it." Maybe it doesn't, but is it more sensible to learn to use a new mechanical device, or to spend that time learning something new about riding without it?

Mechanical devices usually are a means of physically overpowering a horse, or inflicting a higher degree of pain. That kind of approach generally only crops up among people when at least one of the parties isn't thinking creatively. Make sure the horse's size, temperament, or reputation does not become an excuse to not use our smarts.

Some very, very astute riders can use mechanical devices to put the horse in a position for it to discover a new solution to their difficulties. More frequent, mechanical devices greatly complicate things, because they can easily mask the root cause of problems without solving them. If a mechanical device prevents a problem from being expressed though one kind of symptom (a martingale to stop head tossing, for example, or draw reins to keep the horse's head low), the unresolved problem is certain to show up in other ways. That may be teeth grinding, tongue problems, rigid carriage, going behind the bit, and so on. Unresolved problems don't go away—they reappear in a new form. Unfortunately, that may be when we start reaching for a new device to deal with the new symptom. Mechanical devices tend to go along with traveling symptoms.

For example, it's pretty easy to teach a horse there are unpleasant consequences to putting their head where we don't want it to be. We can do this with and without mechanical aids (special rein signals are one way), but it can seem easier on the rider and looks more advanced to use a special device or cue, especially if it requires lots of jargon-filled explanation. However, I question whether a rider is wiser about where a horse's head should be than the horse itself is?

There are many ways to force the horse's head into a fashionable carriage, but that may not help the horse use its back well and therefore allow free leg play even in shortened strides. It is quite possible to teach the horse to disassociate what their head and neck are doing from what its hindquarters and back are doing. This is in stark comparison with horses who adopt a head carriage because it harmonizes with its overall balance and the well-coordinated and free motion of the back.

The head carriage a horse volunteers reflects whether or not the horse has the overall balance we are looking for. Wise riders don't hide that valuable clue by imposing a particular head carriage, any more than good gym teachers would force a gymnast into a body cast to help a student get down a balance beam.

Just like people's arm movements could be signs of good or bad balance, head carriage is a good indicator of how the horse is supporting its center of gravity. Is the rider going to be more able to identify the root problem after the horse's head is locked into place? Making it impossible for the horse to alter its head carriage to express its difficulties may make discovering the root problem all the more difficult.

On the other hand, a horse that volunteers the head carriage we desire must have an awful lot going the way we want. Head carriage can be a sign of success, if it is the result of the horse volunteering the desired head carriage as the best match for its overall balance.

Using a device to prevent a horse from doing things that fairly scream of their discomfort, like gaping mouths (special nosebands) and stiff necks (various draw reins) and wringing tails (deaden the horse's tail nerves chemically or surgically) and poor response to leg aids (whips and spurs), will not solve problems like teeth that need attention or a badly fitting bit, strain on their hocks or backs, a badly fitting saddle, clashing aids, or any of a number of possible causes of distress. I would like to do a study one day on how long after someone started using mechanical devices the horse's vet or other therapy bills start to go up. For those who were very clear on the basic problem, the results would probably be encouraging. For all others, it would probably be very humbling.

Mechanical devices generally just convey a message more powerfully than we could on our own. Mechanical devices send bad messages just as powerfully as good ones. No mechanical device yet made can listen to the horse's side of the conversation, and can never be open to discussion like a person can be. If you are clearly sending the message you mean to send but the horse isn't cooperating, maybe it has a good reason. If the horse acts as if it thinks cooperating will hurt more than not cooperating, you might want to check out why that is.

For example, let's say you're thinking about wearing spurs. My question is: why wouldn't your horse reliably respond to a normal leg aid without them?

There is one time we always wear spurs: when you use a double bridle, spurs are required. However, the idea isn't that a spurred heel is required to overpower two bits. The second bit plus the spur are supposed to be additional tools, like having more instruments in your jazz band, so to speak. Neither the second bit nor the spur is supposed to constitute a higher threat level to the horse. Quite the contrary. They are supposed to demonstrate that you can keep the same level of trust and harmony with more powerful tools as you had with milder ones.

The best riders I have known who compete when required in double bridles and spurs also check that their performance is just as good in lighter bits without spurs at home.

Some horses are just thick skinned, either by their nature or by training. I can understand carrying a whip or spurs with them until they develop their attentiveness and their trust that responding to light communications from the rider will always turn out to be a very comfortable thing to do. This is far more often a matter of using better timing than of getting tougher, since getting tougher rather than more accurate may well have led to the dullness in the first place. A horse who learned tough aids from its very early training may always have doubts on whether light aids are worth attending to. They may never have had the chance to respond to good aids.

Riders who always carry a whip or spurs will never find out how much they are relying on them until they don't carry them. They tend to have horses who cannot be relied upon without them. The big clue that a mechanical device like a whip, spur, or sharp bit has not been used sensibly is that the rider cannot get the horse's cooperation without it, or some substitute for it. If a mechanical device is going to do its job at all, it will not be something the rider comes to depend on. So, the question becomes how quickly you can put it back in storage. If the original problem crops up again as soon as the device is gone for a day or two, it wasn't addressing the right problem anyway.

One situation for which I can agree that having a whip or spur available is the best idea is when the demands are high and there would be a high risk to the horse's well-being of a mistake in getting its feet where they have to be. I can think of situations where the safest thing to do is a dramatic move right when a horse might understandably hesitate. Assuming you are asking for something within the horse's capability, better a crack with the whip or a prick with the spur than an injury. Portuguese bullfighters' horses come to mind for this sort of thing.

Whips can also be used as an extension of our hands. Taps or even pointing with a whip can convey a certain timing or activate certain muscles groups, and a whip can be used like a flexible barrier. Horses with whom whips have been used in this way have no fear of whips at all.

There are horses that are a little sneaky, too. One horse I evented seemed certain to clear any jump you pointed him at, but the owner insisted I wear spurs with him anyway. She was right. Once in three years the horse did make it clear from quite a ways out that he had no intention of jumping one fence, something well within his ability, a perfectly fine obstacle, and indeed it took some serious spur action to get my side of the conversation across to him. Had I not been able to have that kind of conversation with him that one time, he may well have turned into an unreliable jumper just for the sheer mischief of it. If that conversation had started cropping up regularly, it would have been a different situation. As it was, once in three years was sufficient to get the job done.

There is, as the saying goes, "a bit for every mouth." I like to think that means that bits would always be properly fitted to the horses' mouths, not that there is some mechanical device that will finally gain the horse's respect. I want my horse to respect my riding, not my tack box.

I have always found that those who know enough to understand the various mechanical devices well don't need them much. Remember how your teachers said that using crude language was the sign of a limited vocabulary? Same here. As your conversations with your horse exercise your observation skills and expand your conversational possibilities, you may find the tone of your conversation with the horse changes. You may be able to find just the right message to convey, rather than just saying more harshly the same thing that already didn't work.

Using Objective Measurements

Certainly there are unmeasurable aspects to any performance, things that appeal to an aesthetic sense. I am also quite sure that performances in any fine art or sport with high aesthetic appeal are also precise and accurate in ways that are measurable.

In the end, our work with horses is as intuitive as good dancing, but objective measurements can accurately guide and refine our intuitions. Objective measurements are necessary to train our perceptions. They give us a way to check if our intuitions about what the horse is doing and how it is responding to us are in line with reality.

Objective measurements of performance keep us consistent in our dealings with the horse. When we can measure performance accurately and objectively, we will not be nearly as prone to reward a horse for a certain performance simply because we are in a good mood one day, but correct it for essentially the same performance on another day when we are not as cheery. Objective measurements keep us fair to the horse.

Objective measurements help us keep accurate track of progress, letting us identify exactly what is getting better or worse. They also give us a clear picture of patterns that may not be nearly as obvious if we use only our emotion to evaluate performance without measurable standards.

Objective measurements tend to keep us focused on what is, before we jump to what should be. They give us a clear picture of our starting point A, so we can come up with an effective plan to get to our desired point B. We have to find out what simply is before we can effectively get from what is to what we want things to be. You can still get where you want to go without being sure of your start and end points, but you may take some unnecessary detours on the way. Detours are interesting and informative if you have all the time in the world, but they often mean delays and retracing your route. This can be confusing to your horse and hard on your pocketbook.

One very useful objective measurement of the horse's strides is by its hoof-prints. This observation can be especially useful in groundwork and gives the rider a visual idea of what can also be felt under saddle. You can also use this when riding by observing hoofprints the horse left or even getting off the horse and measuring them.

Watch a horse moving in hand, in the round pen, longeing, or at liberty at the walk or trot (the canter works differently). For each stride, watch the spot on the ground where the inside forefoot touches down. Your eye will want to follow the foot as it leaves the ground, but keep your eye on that one hoofprint itself. The hind leg on the same side will land somewhere in vicinity of the hoofprint in a just split second. Note where the hind foot touches down in relation to the hoofprint left by forefoot. The hind foot may land directly over that print, or in front of it, or behind it, or to the inside or to the outside of the print of the forefoot. Look closely, and you can see what is happening each stride.

We are just looking to see what is, before we decide if we like it or not.

Of prime interest to begin with is the consistency of the steps. It is prefer-able that your horse touches its hind foot down consistently, say, two inches behind the print of the forefoot, than that it step beyond that print for a few strides, then step somewhat to the outside, then step shorter again, etc. Certain lengths of stride are required for certain movements, and some peo-ple feel overstepping (also called overtracking) is "better." Stepping directly into the print of the forefoot might be quite a stretch for a naturally short-strided horse and be a very lazy or tight step for a naturally long-strided horse. But a consistent stride needs to become routine and easy before we start looking for other things to happen in addition to a consistent leg play.

Every change in how the hind foot lands in relation to the forefoot, how-ever minor, reflects a change in the horse's hind leg/back/center of gravity con-nections. The most common inconsistency will be that the stride shortens. That shows up as the hind foot landing behind wherever it landed in relation to print of the forefoot in the previous step. Another common inconsistency is for the hind foot to land to one side or the other of the print of the forefoot. What does that tell us about how the horse's hind leg action is operating on its center of gravity? What does that say about its alignment from tail to ears?

A hind leg most likely lands shorter or more out of line on one step than the previous step because of tightness, distraction, stiffness, weakness, or fatigue. There is a reason for the inconsistency, and that reason will influence everything else that happens. There is also very likely a pattern to these inconsistencies.

Establishing a consistent stride at all gaits is much like playing scales on a piano. Irregularities in playing scales (dada, da, da . . . da, dadada, instead of da, da, da, da, da, da, da, da) indicates the piano player hasn't developed equal dexterity in all fingers for all keys on the piano.

An easy diagnostic of complete physical development for a piano player would be even scales. That may not be impressive musically, but all of that player's music will benefit from removing whatever physical limitations showed up as inconsistent scales. A piano player who is relatively weak in, say, the fourth finger on the right hand would be inconsistent in the scales and in every piece of music. A piano player will play everything better when she brings all of the muscles and bones involved up to equal dexterity and strength. Consistency and equal dexterity may be easier to develop initially at a slower tempo than will be possible later. That's why music teachers use adjustable metronomes.

If you make the piano player do scales faster with that lack of dexterity still in place, you will get what you asked for: faster irregular scales. Similarly, even strides in all gaits and basic figures is a diagnostic of even development throughout the horse's body. Making a horse with irregular strides just go faster, perhaps thinking you are getting the horse to go "forward," can easily train in the very tightness that caused the inconsistency in the first place. Trying to fix one symptom of tension by adding more tension or power can also influence the horse's future expectation of what a good solution to your demands will probably be. More to the point would be to get the part of the horse that was tight or sloppy or weak to release, to become coordinated with and as strong as its other parts.

For the horse, inconsistent strides ultimately means the hind legs are not firing equally and consistently. The bag of water/center of gravity will not slosh consistently and the forelegs will be busy accommodating that. So will the horse's head and neck. The most likely reaction will be for a foreleg to slam down earlier than if a hind leg had not withdrawn. This is not the picture of an athlete—or not one that is using itself fully and healthily for the long run.

So developing a horse's full athletic potential starts with identifying any tendencies to move at all irregularly, right down to how each foot operates in each stride. Inconsistencies in the basic footfall can always be traced to some physical limitation, one that may well have a psychological aspect, too. You can't do anything sensible about these inconsistencies until you can identify them both on the ground (visually) and under saddle (your passive seat). There will be a pattern to them for each horse that reveals the kind of gymnastic assistance it needs.

Most often, the root physical limitation is rather localized, especially if you catch it before other compensations start showing up. Just like we start walking and running and sitting normally again when a sore knee heals, all of the various ways a root problem influenced the horse's performance will improve, too, once the root problem is resolved. In NLP terms, this is called "the change that makes a difference."

Once a horse starts moving evenly and therefore rhythmically, it almost always offers a freer stride when it feels its center of gravity is being reliably and consistently supported. An overstep of the hind foot past the print of the same-side forefoot may appear apparently out of the blue, if the horse is built to move that way. Our refined observation skills will help us to encourage that accurately in the horse and to further develop that way of going if that's what we're after.

Once you have identified these inconsistencies, you now have lots of ways to address their root cause(s). Now that you have so many means whereby you can identify small inconsistencies and the patterns in which they show up, and also the tools to help the horse solve them (aids), you might be astounded how many seemingly larger problems simply vanish.

Once you've got your eye trained for objectively measuring the horse's stride at the walk and trot, you can also train your eye for consistent canter strides. Watch where the inside foreleg touches down for one stride. That's the last beat of that stride. The next stride starts with the outside hind, so watch where the outside hind of the next stride lands in relation to the print of the inside fore, and you can tell how long that stride was and how the horse was lined up. Just to give your eye some advance information, a rather average canter stride sets the outside hind leg down about level with where the inside fore was in the previous stride, which is to say the horse gains about one body length each canter stride. Lazy or tense canters may well leave the outside hind a good deal behind the print of the inside fore, whereas a smart canter may well have the outside hind land well in front of the print of the inside fore. A gallop most certainly will.

You can expect that the outside hind would land a bit to the side of the print of the inside fore at the canter, unless the horse is carrying its hips to the inside, which is not unusual. Again, we are looking for first is consistency rather than a specific performance. You will soon get a sense of your horse's average gaits.

Objective measurements are necessary starting points to plan and evaluate the horse's gymnastic development. Measuring hoofprints is not the complete story, but it is an excellent and easily visible indicator from which we can draw good conclusions about how we can help a horse develop its full abilities. It is very worthwhile to compare the horse's footfall in each direction, as well as how they change in turns in either direction. This can tell you much about how evenly the horse is developing each side's suppleness and dexterity. For example, let's say you find one of your horse's hind legs commonly shortens under certain conditions, say, right turns. You can then figure out exercises to improve its range of motion, dexterity, and suppleness and how to communicate the way you want your horse to use itself in those exercises. You will also discover the many ways the horse can tell you if you are on the right track or not, such as its responsiveness to aids and better balance and more fluid gaits, and more consistent hoof placement.

This can bring a new point of interest to your riding, and a new source of satisfaction. You can know for a fact your horse is improving because of the insight, knowledge, and attention you bring to your riding in any sport.

CHAPTER 11

Using What We Know Now

The conversation between rider . . . and horse is never-ending; always,
during every stride, the rider asks little questions. The horse may query,
the rider will explain, the horse understand and improve his answers day by
day, until gradually the mutual conversation reaches higher and higher levels
and becomes more interesting, light, and pleasant to both participants.
—Henry Wynmalen

Learning any art form or skill is a process of learning
how to ask questions clearly and with increasing depth.
—Carol Wiley

Now we know quite a bit about our own physical patterns, our learning patterns, how we can communicate to the horse by how it experiences us as riders, and how to discover the horse's current physical patterns. We have a greater sense of how the horse experiences being ridden and how that can be used as a basis for communication. We can put this all together to communicate effectively and securely, using the horse's motion so our aids improve our seat and make the job we want done as easy as possible for the horse to do. One example of how we could use this information is to look at a basic element of riding, like changing gaits. Another example is using the horse's alignment from tail to ears to diagnose and influence its overall gymnastic development.

PHASES AND THE TRANSITIONS
BETWEEN THE GAITS

We can teach the horse any signals we like to mean whatever gaits we like, and I agree that cues and signals (conditioned responses) work well to a point. But using conditioned responses to cues has some basic disadvantages in comparison with using to our advantage what the horse is already doing anyway. Rather than adding whatever set of signals we decide we like to what the horse must learn, we can just activate or delay what particular feet are doing anyway.

If we can convey when we want particular feet to speed up or slow down, our aids become dance-like communications that every horse can understand easily. Even horses that have never been ridden before can easily understand what you want them to do, if you understand that well enough yourself. The better the rider understands what the horse is already doing and about to do next in any gait, the easier it will be to convey to the horse how we would like to change things.

For example, changing gaits is a matter of changing the horse's footfall more than changing the horse's speed. Look at the chart on page 200, and you will see that some phases of each gait are very similar to phases in other gaits. These are the most opportune moments to make transitions between the gaits. You can easily ask any horse for any gait if you know which foot you want to speed up or slow down to create that new footfall. When you time your aids well, the horse can understand you as easily as you can understand a good dance partner. The horse has the least work to do to change from one footfall (gait) to another, which is how they generally like to go about things. Another benefit is that our aids help to improve our seat by working with the horse's movement, rather than disturbing our seat by working against it.

For example, we can use certain phases of the canter for neat transitions into and out of the other gaits. Horses have more than way to move into and out of the canter, so we can use canter transitions to see that there are many ways to change gaits by using rather small changes in footfall.

Notice that there is a lot of similarity between the sixth and seventh walk phases and the second and third canter phases. All it takes to change the sixth

Walk Footfall	Walk Phases	Trot Footfall	Trot Phases	Canter Footfall	Canter Phases
	(1) inside hind + inside fore				
(1) outside hind	(2) inside hind + inside fore + outside hind			(1) outside hind	(1) outside hind
	(3) inside fore + outside hind	(1) inside fore + outside hind	(1) inside fore + outside hind	(2) inside hind + outside fore	(2) outside hind + inside hind + outside fore
(2) outside fore	(4) inside fore + outside hind + outside fore				
	(5) outside hind + outside fore	(2) suspension	(2) suspension		(3) inside hind + outside fore
(3) inside hind	(6) outside hind + outside fore + inside hind				
	(7) outside fore + inside hind	(3) outside fore + inside hind	(3) outside fore + inside hind		
(4) inside fore	(8) outside fore + inside hind + inside fore			(3) inside fore	(4) inside hind + outside fore + inside fore
					(5) inside fore
		(4) suspension	(4) suspension		(6) suspension

or seventh phase of the walk into a canter is for the outside hind to push off a bit more strongly and the inside fore to touch down a bit farther forward. Voila! the fourth phase of a canter! The next stride will be a complete canter stride, with the outside hind as the first beat as usual. It is easy to imagine an outside leg aid and a bit of release on the inside rein at that moment conveying the canter footfall to the horse.

There is more than one way to ride easy canter transitions. As the chart shows, there are other phases of the canter and of the walk that have the same two or three feet on the ground. These could all be opportune moments for easy canter/walk and walk/canter transitions. Which phases you choose to use depends on which canter lead you want and whether you feel it will be easier to activate or delay a particular leg.

For example, phase two of the walk is ripe for a canter on the outside lead, needing only an extra push from the hind legs and a reach with the outside fore to make a counter-canter out of a walk. The canter's third phase looks a lot like the walk's third and seventh phases. The horse would have an easy time making a canter/walk transition at that moment, too.

It is easy for a horse to make one kind of trot/canter transition from the third phase of the trot (outside hind and inside fore in flight) by quickening the inside foreleg touchdown and keeping the outside hind leg in flight a bit longer than for a trot. This breaks the in-flight diagonal pair out of its two-beat trot action and creates a three-legged support phase: inside hind, outside fore, and inside fore. Voila! we have the fourth phase of the canter again. So if you want a canter on the left lead out of the trot, one way to do that is to nudge the horse forward onto its left fore just as it is reaching forward with its left fore anyway. Horses often use this kind of canter transition, especially when they are somewhat on their forehand, like many young horses and horses at liberty.

Canter/trot transitions fairly beg to be done in the third phase of the canter. The horse already has a diagonal pair of legs on the ground, ready to make the next stride a trot stride. Hold that diagonal pair on the ground a bit, reduce the horse's body speed a bit, ask the inside fore in flight not to touch down quite yet, and the outside hind leg can match up with it to make a diagonal

Just finishing the sixth phase of the walk and moving into the seventh walk phase. Notice how similar this moment of the walk is to . . .

. . . moving from the third phase into the fourth phase of the canter. A bit more push from the left hind and a bit more reach with the right fore, and the walk is easily changed into a canter. Study lots of photos and film to find other phases when it would be easiest to change between the gaits.

pair for the next step to become a good, forward-moving trot. This hints at why downward transitions work better when you don't limit yourself to rein aids that act like brakes. Speaking to specific feet to change footfall is a much more direct pathway than just using speed. Bonus question: Are there other ways to change between the two-beat trot and a three-beat canter?

Transitions to the halt are obviously easiest at any phase that already has the most legs on the ground, ready to accept more weight. More comfortable halts come from the horse shifting its weight to the hindquarters, leaving the forelegs with less weight to carry than when the horse brakes to a halt by bracing its forelegs. It is possible to create a halt out of a phase of suspension just by slamming all four legs down at once, but those are what you might call back busters. They are hard on horse and rider, but they will get you stopped.

Bonus questions: which phases of each gait look like a good time to get to a halt? A sliding stop? What legs would you want to speed up or slow down? How would you convey that to the horse?

Any rider who has done a couple walk/trot transitions probably already knows a lot more about this than they realize. However, the kick-trot sequence that often goes along with our first trots can easily overshadow what we felt happening as the horse made the transition. This sets the stage to become body blind to the horse's main means of communication to the rider—its motion—in favor of kicking with legs and pulling with reins, however gently. I call this "riding handsey-heelsey," even when the aids are as gentle as can be.

Exploring how timing your aids with a specific leg motion changes results can refine your search images for gaits and transitions, by sharpening your attention to events and their outcomes. As you repeat your experiments, you will discover that timing is more effective than force and that your horse starts becoming more attentive, too. You might find that using the horse's motion up to, during, and beyond the transitions improves your seat through the transitions, too. This counters a common tendency to lock up during transitions and relax (maybe) after the horse has done what we asked. Staying tuned in to footfall during transitions, not just before and after them, will help keep your seat moving freely. That in itself makes the job easier for the horse and also helps your aids work with the horse's motion. Transitions might be the most worthwhile conversations you have with your horse.

LATERAL FLEXION

Flexing the horse's spine laterally, causing the horse to adopt a convex curve on one side and a concave curve on the other side, is one form of lateral flexion. Sometimes this is called bending the horse around the rider's inside leg. The convex side is called the outside, and the concave side is called the inside. The more lateral flexion, the more lengthened the outside of the horse is relative to its inside. The relative lengthening of the outside of the horse can help supple and release any tensions or contractions on that side of the horse, just like some lateral yoga stretches do for people. The relative lengthening on the outside can be worth gold. It is the real point of lateral flexion.

Good lateral flexion develops the horse's ability to release tensions and to release forward toward the bit on both sides of its body, concentrating on one side (the outside) at a time. That can be especially useful for a horse just getting into work, since we want to supple the horse and release any constraints in both sides of its body before we start strength or agility training. Doing strengthening work before thoroughly suppling the horse makes whatever is already strong stronger, but leaves tensions in place and continues to bypass what is weak or slack.

Lateral flexion is more than flexing a horse's neck to one side or the other, and therefore is not a matter of rein aids. Neck flexions are sometimes thought to supple a horse, but just like in people, ninety-nine times out of a hundred neck stiffness is a symptom of problems elsewhere. Lateral flexion that doesn't use flexion all along the horse's spine overlooks the full gymnastic benefit of lateral flexion to the horse's whole body. Aside from problems that come from teaching a horse to disassociate its neck from its body, flexing just the neck is about as valuable as doing yoga from the neck up only. Fix the problems elsewhere that underlie a tense neck, and the neck stiffness will disappear like magic.

We use lateral flexion to equalize the horse's development on both sides, with the aim of making it as ambidextrous as possible. A horse that can flex laterally equally well on both sides has removed any limitations to moving straightly and using itself equally well in any direction. Since no horse (or person) is naturally equally dexterous on both sides, lateral flexion is part of every well-trained horse's suppling program. A horse that is well suppled on both sides is the horse that can move truly straightly, so the power of its hindquarters operates directly toward the center of gravity. So we use lateral flexion to improve straightness, just like you might flex a crooked stick back and forth to straighten it.

Lateral flexion is great for diagnosing how one side of the horse's body is developing in comparison with the other side. If a horse has more trouble with lateral flexion to one side than the other, something must be tight or slack or isolated somewhere. A horse that can flex laterally throughout its body equally well in both directions must be pretty thoroughly supple and dexterous, much more ready for whatever the rider might ask than if some stiffness or weakness remains somewhere. Our strengthening work is more beneficial for the entire horse after the horse is suppled on both sides of its body. If the horse's dexterity is not developed reasonably equally before strength or endurance training begins, the horse will continue to rely on the parts it already uses more and therefore may wear out prematurely.

To use the horse's power efficiently, the horse's entire spine should adopt the same line as the line the horse is traveling. The horse's hind feet would land in line with the forefeet, not to one side or the other, on both straight lines and curves. If the horse's hind legs work off to the side of the center of gravity, they are not pushing the horse's body forward directly, and the inside and outside legs are not being used equally well. One side working harder than the other will take its toll over time.

If you looked at a horse from above and drew an imaginary line across the horse's hips and another across its shoulders, those lines would be parallel to each other in a horse that is straight from tail to ears and traveling straight forward. For a horse that has its spine laterally flexed equally along its length, as when it is traveling a curve, those two lines would angle like spokes on a

The real point of lateral flexion is to lengthen the outside of the horse's body evenly from hoof to nose, as shown here at the half pass. A horse that can flex laterally equally well on both sides is thoroughly supple and can use its natural talents to the fullest.

Misalignment instead of flexion.

Lateral flexion isn't just for the dressage arena!

wheel. The point at which the two imaginary lines would eventually meet is the center of the circle or turn the horse is making.

If the horse is evenly flexed along its spine, the horse's inside hip is closer to its inside shoulder and its outside hip is farther away from its outside shoulder. The rule of thumb is that the rider's hips should be parallel with the horse's hips, and the rider's shoulders should be parallel with the horse's shoulders. On a laterally flexed horse, then, the rider's inside hip would be more forward than on a straight horse, and the rider's outside shoulder would be more forward than on a straight horse.

A rider can move his rib cage and hips in opposite directions like this, if the spine remains stacked up and the rider's front stays quite open from collarbones to knees. Tipping to the side more than the horse, pulling a shoulder down, drawing a hip up or back, or shifting the rib cage off center from the pelvis aren't at all the same as rotating around an aligned spine.

Happily, since seat aids create leg aids, this more forward-moving inside hip (active seat aid) goes nicely with the rider lengthening into the inside stirrup (active leg aid) and the horse's inside hind reaching more forward under the horse's belly in lateral flexion. Or, looking at things another way, the rider's outside leg behind the girth (a unilateral leg aid) can help flex the horse's spine laterally. This is somewhat different than shifting the hindquarters or the whole horse sideways as in a turn on the forehand or some lateral movements. A laterally flexed horse's inside hip and hind foot are somewhat more forward than its outside hip and hind foot, which itself helps the rider create the desired active inside seat and leg aids. Once again, we see the potential for a virtuous cycle in which the harmoniously combined aids give the horse the message to swing the inside hind leg more forward and at least not let the hindquarters step to the outside, and that in turn makes it easier for the rider to continue the appropriate aids.

Lateral flexion evenly throughout the horse's spine from tail to ears also goes nicely with the rider's outside shoulder being somewhat in advance of her inside shoulder. Lateral flexion like this requires letting the outside foot lengthen away from the outside shoulder, even the outside eye, for both horse and rider. A rider's relatively advanced outside shoulder helps keep the rider's outside hand from restricting the horse's stretch on the outside, too. A horse that seeks the bit would lengthen the outside of its body in response to this arrangement.

The tighter the turn, the more lengthened and convex the outside of the horse would be, and the more the outside foot would have to lengthen away from the outside shoulder and even ear. Bonus questions: what would it mean if the horse wasn't as good at lengthening the outside of its body going in one direction as going the other way? How would the horse experience a rider who wasn't lengthening one side of his body as well as the other?

It is not uncommon for riders to draw the inside hip back along with the inside shoulder when they look for a turn, which makes the rider's platform oppose the horse bringing its inside hip forward. The inside hind may not swing forward far enough to lend much support to the center of gravity. A horse can turn like that, but not with even lateral flexion through its spine and its full power operating directly on the center of gravity. This platform fault will also make the leg aids harder to use than they need be, as platform problems always do.

This rotation around an upright spine that goes along with lateral flexion is not a large movement even for spins, rollbacks, and pirouettes—just enough to agree with the lateral flexion needed. Nor are we talking about adopting a pose that is supposed to convey something to the horse magically, for that is not movement. A horse who is evenly suppled on both sides of its body has better overall dexterity, and has been given the opportunity to learn that lateral flexion makes many of its jobs easier. Lateral flexion keeps the horse's alignment from tail to ears in agreement with its line of travel, keeps the center of gravity more directly under the horse's spine, and thus evens the load on its inside and outside legs. It also makes more use of the hind leg(s) to support the combined horse/rider weight, lending greater freedom to the forelegs. In the long run, that is easier on the horse than misalignment with the horse's center of gravity well to one side or the other, which requires the horse to prop itself up with a foreleg. As the horse's suppleness develops, the horse may well begin to volunteer this way of going, and suggest the appropriate seat to the rider if the rider is using the horse's motion well. This is another reason it is best to learn to ride on a well-trained horse, which means much more than a horse that is well versed in a certain set of cues.

On a horse with well-developed lateral flexion, you can tell how large or small a turn or circle the horse is making even with your eyes closed, just by how much lateral flexion the horse has and how that changes the way the horse carries you.

"This Could Take Years!!"

No, it takes no time at all to tune in to what your horse is doing. Doing that may make riding a source of endless fascination, though.

I can almost hear the lightbulbs switching on for some riders when they start learning about gait mechanics and the potential for the gymnastic benefits for horses of good riding. Some people can get very involved with gait and transition analysis, lateral flexion as a first step in developing a horse equally well on both sides, and training for gymnastic benefits. This information hardly exhausts the discussion. I applaud those who learn these skills by studying the many resources available, but not everyone works best that way. Not a problem.

You may well discover moments as you ride when your aids work perfectly with the horse's motion and phases seemingly by chance, and that's terrific. That is how we often learn the most. As the saying goes, though, chance favors the prepared mind, so it may be worth some book and film time, too. Knowing gait mechanics and lateral flexion may be useful to clarify why things worked better in practice one time than another time. It is quite sufficient to know that there are moments in each stride when it is easiest for the horse to do what we want it to do next and that it is easy to convey that to the horse by addressing specific feet. Just knowing these moments are there, literally under your nose, is likely to develop your sensitivity to them.

Many riders have discovered these moments without perhaps having the words to describe them. They can feel the moment a horse is ready to bounce into a lovely canter, or that the horse is more awkward at some tasks than others, without having to write a thesis about it first. They know that the timing of their aids makes a difference in how well the horse goes. That seems more to the point than being able to describe it but not to ride it. Learning more about the horse's movement and gymnastic development can clarify your physical experience, but it cannot substitute for it. Experience is by far the best teacher. Simply stay tuned into the horse's footfall prior to and during transitions and how easily a horse uses either side of its body. You will soon know everything you need to know.

For example, you can experiment with using particular phases for transitions quite easily. Try tuning in to the moment when each hind leg is swinging forward at the trot. Ask for a canter once just as the inside hind is swinging forward, and note what happens. Then, try asking for the canter when the outside hind is swinging forward, and see what happens. What happens if you ask when the inside hind is on the ground? Or when the outside hind is on the ground? How do different rein aids influence the horse's response to your leg aids? Repeat each experiment as interesting. You could set up some experiments about the timing of your aids for any transitions or movements that interest you. Certainly attending to the horse's alignment during these experiments will show you how that promotes the work or not, as the case may be. The proof is in the horse's quality of work.

Every step a horse takes can be used as an educational conversation. Horses will gladly teach us everything we need to know about them very easily if we let them, and if we acknowledge how much we have learned without knowing we learned it. We can look things up in a book to help us imagine which legs activated and when and how, but that study will be most effective when it refers to our physical experience.

I find it quite successful in the long run for riders to develop their skill at identifying how their interface with the horse can work with or against the horse's movement while being longed. Learning to longe horses well can also teach riders much about the horse's gait mechanics and psychology before they are expected to apply this knowledge under saddle.

The leadership role riders must adopt when we start telling the horse what to do has its duties. Leadership does put the greater burden of understanding on the rider, which is where I think it belongs. We are supposed to be the smart ones in the partnership, since we are the ones who get to say what to do.

So, developing ever-finer understanding of what the horse is doing, how the horse experiences us, and how we help the horse's physical well-being makes sensible, reality-based, two-sided body language conversations under saddle more interesting, understandable, healthier, and performance-enhancing for horses in any sport.

Luckily, we are designed by Nature with any number of built-in tools to identify and remove limitations of our horses' performance, so this should be right up our alley as humans. What is especially neat is that exactly the same things that help us as riders help our horses as athletes.

When you think about it, how could it be otherwise?

SUMMARY

One of the classical masters, Gustav Steinbrecht, said all riding can be explained in eight words: "Ride your horse forward and keep it straight." We can gymnasticize a horse well enough that it can easily be consistently active and lined up from tail to ears, equally supple, strong, and dexterous throughout its body. That will surely reward us with horses who can carry us easily and comfortably, promptly understand and respond to all of our aids equally well, and use its talents to their fullest in the best possible health for the longest period of time.

Making the horse's even pace and good alignment from tail to ears your top priority before you start working on the specifics of your favorite sport just ensures that your horse will be able to use its talents to the fullest. Riding with this priority may require an essential mental shift at first, but developing yourself and the horse evenly and spreading the burden of work fairly over its skeleton and muscles is bound to improve performance in any sport. Just as yoga and other body work practices, such as Alexander Technique, Pilates, yoga, and such, concentrate on developing symmetry and suppleness to make all other activities easier and more healthful, attending to your own and your horse's symmetrical development will pay off in the long run. You will avoid having ever to swallow the bitter pill of relinquishing the dream that you first starting riding to fulfill.

Going about things with your horse's gymnastic development as a top priority adds a new level of interest to even the slowest trail ride and a new level of security and success in ever more challenging performances.

From a competitive point of view, riding to improve your horse's gymnastic development adds an aspect of interest and progress to competitions that can otherwise become boringly repetitive, especially since not solving your horse' gymnastic limitations tends to keep you at the same level of performance for a long time. Even the most enthusiastic riders can only ride so many of the same kinds of jump courses, reining patterns, or trails before they start asking themselves, "Is that all there is?" A common response to that is to start exploring new riding sports. While I thoroughly applaud riders who explore every aspect of riding, it may be more worthwhile to explore what is keeping your performance at a certain plateau in a sport you already know well. With that solved, applying your new skills to new sports will be that much easier and successful.

Like the boy in the Sufi story that opened this book, we have been given the tools we need to gain a thorough understanding of whatever sport we like. Having explored a few skills to gain of clear observation and clear pathways of communication for yourself and your horse, you can knowledgeably evaluate where you are at this point and how to get where you want to go. You can find many ways to identify and develop your talents in whatever sport you pursue with your horse today or next year. Along the way, you will surely discover talents you did not realize you had.

There are many forms of good horsemanship, but seeing your horse benefit from your riding is the blue ribbon we all really want. We know in our hearts if we are achieving that, whether there is an official judge around to see it or not. What can observers tell you that you and your horse don't really already know, anyway?

I wish you the very best on your explorations and hope you and your horses enjoy the adventures you undertake for many years to come. Let me know how it's working at www.seamlessseat.com.

INDEX